THE BALCONY GARDENER

THE BALCONY GARDENER
CREATIVE IDEAS FOR SMALL SPACES

Isabelle Palmer

CICO BOOKS
LONDON NEW YORK

*To my Grandmother, always my
inspiration & always in my heart*

This edition published in 2018 by CICO Books
An imprint of Ryland Peters & Small Ltd
20–21 Jockey's Fields
London WC1R 4BW
341 E 116th St.,
New York, NY 10029

www.rylandpeters.com

10 9 8 7 6 5 4 3 2 1

First published in 2012 by CICO Books
Text © Isabelle Palmer 2012
Design and photography © CICO Books 2012

A CIP catalog record for this book is
available from the Library of Congress
and the British Library.

ISBN: 978 1 78249 552 9

Printed in China

Editor: Caroline West
Designer: Ashley Western
Photographers: Amanda Darcy
and Keiko Oikawa
Stylist: Marisa Daly

CONTENTS

INTRODUCTION

I started *The Balcony Gardener* because of my difficulties in finding gardening products and plants suitable for my own small outdoor spaces. I wanted to make the most of my balconies and create an area where I could sit, look around, relax, and grow my own little bit of green in the midst of the city. Growing different types of shrubs, flowers, herbs, and small vegetables in such a small space has been a joy. Looking out on the flora and visiting fauna is not only uplifting—my garden is also a source of great pride. For this reason, I would like to encourage others to create an area where they can relax at the end of a long day and feel those benefits too.

New developments in gardening products also mean that gardeners can use any available space very efficiently, so now you can have your own garden even on a wall or windowsill. In this book, I have tried to give some helpful advice as a starting point to inspire you on your own horticultural journey, and I hope it helps.

Getting started

We all live busy lives and, if you have never had a garden before, it can be a daunting thought not knowing where to begin. I know that this was how I felt initially and, looking back, my balcony garden started out as not much more than two pot plants. So, I would suggest that you start small. By small, I mean growing easy-care and low-maintenance plants at first to start to build the foundations of what you want to achieve. There is nothing worse than spending lots of money and seeing everything die in front of your eyes. This will certainly dampen any hopes and dreams you may have, but, in saying that, you don't have to be especially skillful to create a garden. You simply have to appreciate that plants are living things, which means they need water, food and light, a little tender loving care, and a habitat in which they can thrive. This may sound rather glib, but that really is all there is to it.

Designing your outdoor space

By carefully selecting plants that you like and which complement each other, as well as sourcing contemporary and vintage accessories to reflect your tastes, you, too, can create the outdoor space you deserve. So, turn your garden into an extension of your home, and pay as much attention to the decorative features as to the planting. Consider, for example, how you might include outdoor lighting, furnishings, and other items to create a special oasis of your own. If you are on a budget you can be thrifty and reuse old cans, wooden crates, and even old pallets, as well as antique or thrift (charity) store finds.

Growing your own

The growing popularity of gardening, especially the desire to "grow-your-own," reflects a positive shift in values. For many gardeners, growing vegetables and herbs is a form of self-sufficiency, and what nicer way could there be to enhance your life than cutting home-grown herbs for cooking or inventing a dish from what you've grown. I personally love entertaining, particularly when using ingredients in my cooking that I have grown myself.

Record your progress

It's a good idea to take photos of every season once you've got started; believe me, there is nothing better than documenting how you have grown in knowledge and practice, however narcissistic this may seem. I don't believe a year goes by in which I don't adapt an idea or experiment in some way. I don't think you can ever know everything about gardening, but that to me is the joy—forever being surprised!

Isabelle Palmer

CHAPTER 1

THE BASICS

This is where to begin if you're a first-time gardener. Here, I have outlined the basic techniques that you will need to follow in order to start balcony gardening. I show you how to choose and plant up your containers and care for your plants, as well as how to combine plant colors successfully. I explain how you can enhance your urban space with those extra-special finishing touches to make it truly your own. Once you have mastered these basics, you can go on to create your ideal ornamental garden or even a mini-allotment.

Before designing and planting a balcony or roof-top garden, think carefully about the style you'd prefer, how often you'll entertain there, and whether you may want to grow some vegetables or herbs. But, most importantly, consider how much time you will be able to give in order to maintain your new urban oasis.

ESSENTIALS BEFORE YOU BEGIN

One of the first things I say to people considering a balcony or roof garden is that it's essential to check with a qualified architect or structural engineer first to find out how much weight your roof can take and whether planning permission is needed. You'll also have to ascertain whether your balcony or roof garden is waterproof. This may sound strict, but it's worth following the correct regulations initially to avoid paying for the damage if, for example, you flood your home or make the roof or balcony collapse under the weight of heavy containers. Ideally, position containers on the perimeter of a balcony or roof garden near load-bearing walls or over a load-bearing beam or joist.

Dreams and possibilities
You will then need to give some thought to the plants that will actually thrive there, as well as how you want to use your new outdoor space. The points I've outlined here are not intended to be rules because there are always exceptions (and I don't think that being too stringent makes for much gardening enjoyment). However, plants are living things and following these guidelines will help your garden flourish:

Be selective Choose containers that create focal points and spend money on a couple of larger containers rather than on lots of smaller ones. Too many plants or ornaments can make a small space look overcrowded.

Think about light When container gardening, tailor your planting to the available light. If you have low levels of sunlight, use shade-tolerant plants with lush foliage such as hostas, heucheras, ivy, and grasses.

Create a backdrop Start with evergreen plants such as box and sweet bay. Lavender also provides a year-round green base, but it won't flower all the time. Then, add your favorite colors with flowering perennials such as *Agapanthus*, bleeding heart, campanula, and clematis that have a long blooming period and will come back next year.

Use odd numbers Planting in odd numbers gives the most aesthetically pleasing results, so plant one, three, or five plants in a container.

Restrict the color palette Don't overdo the number of colors in a planting scheme; it will look too busy and make your garden look smaller.

Start with herbs It may not be possible to grow an entire vegetable patch, but start with a small container or window box packed with your favorite herbs or salads. Not only do you get the satisfaction of growing your own produce but these crops can also be used in cooking. Mint, chives, rosemary, parsley, and a salad mix are good varieties to start with.

Grow vegetables Once you've mastered herbs, move on to other crops. Vegetables such as tomatoes, salad onions, carrots, eggplants (aubergines), beans, cabbages, potatoes, and radishes, as well as fruits like strawberries, will all thrive. Remember that the amount of sunlight will influence what you can grow.

Care and maintenance Whether you are growing ornamental or edible plants (or both), follow regular watering and feeding routines to get the best results.

ESSENTIAL KIT

Part of the fun of gardening is choosing gardening tools and equipment and then pottering around your roof terrace or balcony. Obviously, the list of essential tools is not as extensive as for a garden on the ground, but here I've suggested items that I've found the most useful.

Watering cans and garden hoses

You'll probably find that a couple of smaller watering cans are more useful than one large one, which will be heavy to lift when full of water. A watering can with a long spout can also be useful in helping you reach in between plants in a larger container. You'll probably need a rose attachment to deliver a softer shower when watering seeds or delicate plants like seedlings or annuals. It's also a good idea to choose a watering can that you find easy to carry because you'll be spending a lot of time watering your plants in summer. You can, of course, water plants with a garden hose. If you don't have an outdoor tap for the hose, then you can buy special hose attachments to fit on indoor taps.

Trowels and hand forks

These are vital tools for the balcony gardener; you'll be turning to them time and again for breaking up potting mix, digging out holes for new plants, and weeding. You can buy trowels and hand forks with wooden or plastic handles, but invest in stainless-steel tools if possible because they are more effective. Lastly, and perhaps most importantly, try out the tools in the shop first to find out which ones are the easiest to handle. My first trowel and hand fork are still in their packaging because they were so uncomfortable to use.

Hand pruners

Even on a balcony or roof terrace, there will be wayward plants that need trimming or cutting back, so a good pair of hand pruners (secateurs) is absolutely essential. If you are growing bamboo or laurel as screening plants, roses in pots, or evergreens such as box or holly, then at some stage these will need tidying up, pruning, or shaping.

A PAIR OF GLOVES Wear a pair of gardening gloves when you are handling potting mix and pruning plants, for example. You can, of course, wear a very practical, rather utilitarian-looking pair of gloves, but there are some beautifully patterned ones available that make garden pottering much more stylish.

Seed-sowing equipment

When growing vegetables or herbs, always buy good-quality, preferably organic, seed so that your produce is free from chemicals. Also buy some coir pots for sowing your seeds in, as these are more environmentally friendly than plastic pots and polystyrene plant trays—they simply rot down in the potting mix when you transplant the young plants to their more permanent containers.

Brackets for window boxes

When suspending window boxes and troughs from a balcony, make sure that they are securely fixed. Always hang the box or trough on the inside of the balcony and not over the edge where they could fall and injure someone. You can buy adjustable balcony brackets to match the filled weight of the window box: small brackets for a small box (weighing 44lb/20kg) and large brackets for a large box (weighing 88lb/40kg). Also available are balcony hooks for both normal and wide balcony ledges, as well as wall hooks.

Plant labels and other useful items

Labels are indispensable, especially if you are going to forget the names of the plants or seeds you've just planted. I suggest you make using labels a part of your planting routine, so that you automatically insert a label (written in indelible pen) in the pot as soon as you've finished. There is no need for plastic labels, either; why not use metal, copper, or slate ones, which are much more decorative? Consider also raising your containers slightly off the "ground" with special pot "feet." Not only do these allow for extra drainage, but they may also help deter slugs. Other useful items include string or twine, wooden post supports, and metal wire for tying in plants, as well as a trug for harvesting crops.

Spray bottles

Use plastic spray bottles to mist plants indoors and tackle unwelcome pests and diseases with organic chemical products. For safety's sake, label the bottles with their uses and always follow the manufacturer's instructions carefully.

I think that one of the most exciting aspects of a "non-traditional" garden is the fun you can have choosing, **creating,** and **arranging** containers. You can afford to play around with various layouts, **colors,** heights, and **combinations** while creating your own **green space.**

CHOOSING AND PREPARING POTS

When choosing and arranging any type of container, consider the size of the available space, as well as what colors work well together. This stage is an opportunity to experiment with different materials, textures, colors, and shades. In general, if you have a small space to fill, then opt for one large pot or a variety of smaller containers made from a similar material or color, so that the space looks well filled and abundant, but not too cramped. Here, I've outlined a few key points to help you when choosing your containers:

Container size Will your choice of container fit the available space? As a general rule, the bigger, the better. So, try to find the deepest containers you can, but which will not be overly heavy when filled with potting mix— this will help reduce the amount of watering and extra feeding you'll need to do.

Moving containers Consider how you will transport the containers to your balcony or roof garden and if they will need moving around once there. You can use a wheeled trolley to move larger pots. Where possible, move the container to its final location before planting.

Grouping containers When arranging your planters in groups, it is more aesthetically pleasing to have containers of different heights, and place the taller ones at the back (as you might arrange plants in a border).

GIVING TERRACOTTA AN AGED LOOK If you like the idea of using traditional terracotta containers but don't have the luxury of waiting for them to weather, then why not age them artificially yourself? You can do this by applying plain yogurt to the surface of the terracotta with a sponge. This encourages lichens and mosses to grow, making your container seem older than it actually is. To create uneven (and therefore more realistic-looking) effects, vary the amount of yogurt over the surface of the terracotta pot.

Storing terracotta pots

Matching plants to pots Check that the containers are large enough to accommodate the selection of plants you wish to grow.

Container choices

There are containers in a range of shapes and sizes to suit different budgets, from the exceedingly expensive through to the relatively low in price. They are also available in lots of interesting materials, including terracotta, wood, wicker, metal (it is best to use lead-effect for older properties, and stainless steel or galvanized zinc for modern ones), ceramic in a range of colors (which are ideal for creating color-themed displays), and stone. If you opt for terracotta or stone containers, then check that they won't be too heavy for the weight-bearing capacity of your balcony or roof garden. You'll also have to check that any imitation terracotta or stone pots are properly frost-proof.

If weight is an issue, then opt for fiberglass containers that look convincingly like traditional materials but are much lighter, making them ideal for gardens in the sky. Remember that containers made from non-porous materials such as metal, plastic, and fiberglass will lose less moisture than those made from porous terracotta. Wire baskets can also look attractive, either as a container for other small pots or lined with coir fiber or moss (like a hanging basket) and planted up themselves.

As well as store-bought containers, you can also use recycled items like olive oil cans, tin baths, and vintage fruit crates, as long as they are prepared properly first.

All in the preparation

If you prepare your containers thoroughly, your plants will reward you with abundant flowers and crops.

Clean the container Use a stiff-bristled brush to give the inside and outside of the container a good scrub with some warm, soapy water before planting up.

Add drainage holes All containers must have drainage holes to prevent the plants from becoming waterlogged. You can make drainage holes with a drill or with a hammer and heavy-duty nail.

Use drainage material Cover the drainage holes with some broken pieces of terracotta pot (or "crocks"), small stones, or small pieces of polystyrene—old plant trays are ideal for this and, being lighter, will help to keep down the weight of the pot.

Line the container If the container is made from a porous material such as wood or wicker, prevent it rotting by lining with plastic sheeting fixed in place with staples. Line recycled containers such as wirework baskets with moss or coir fiber first .

Drainage holes

Terracotta "crocks"

Puncturing drainage holes

When you visit your local garden center, you will inevitably be greeted by stacks of plastic bags filled with different types of potting mix for container planting. This can all seem rather confusing, especially if you are a beginner, so I've put together some helpful tips on how to choose the right potting mix for your plants' needs.

ALL ABOUT POTTING MIX

There are basically two types of potting mix: soil-based and soil-less (usually either peat- or peat-substitute-based). Choosing the right mix for the job is vital for the long-term health of your plants and so it's important to understand the differences between the mixes. The following will help you make an informed choice:

Soil-based potting mixes Growing mediums that contain soil are a mixture of loam, peat, sharp sand, and fertilizers. They hold plants firmly in place and retain moisture well, but this can be a disadvantage with large containers where weight is an issue. There are three types of soil-based potting mix: a light, low-nutrient mix, ideal for seeds and young plants; a slightly heavier mix for potting on young plants; and, finally, a richer mix for mature plants and shrubs that will be growing permanently in pots.

Soil-less potting mixes Since these mixes don't contain any soil, they are much lighter than soil-based potting mixes and you should find them to be perfectly adequate for most types of plant. They are traditionally based on peat, so, if you are at all concerned about the environmental impact of removing peat from bogs, then I advise you to choose a soil-less potting mix made from a peat-substitute such as coir fiber.

These substitutes are now nearly as good as peat. However, the main drawback with peat-based and peat-substitute-based potting mixes is that they tend to dry out easily and are very difficult to rehydrate once dry (a problem that is exacerbated by the windy conditions on top of a balcony or roof garden). For this reason, it's a good idea to add a sprinkling of moisture-retaining granules to the potting mix when planting up your containers.

Sempervivums

SPECIALTY POTTING MIXES It is possible to buy potting mixes for specific purposes. These include container potting mixes for pots and window boxes, which may be a better option for the balcony gardener because they already contain moisture-retaining granules. You can also buy ericaceous potting mixes that are lime-free, making them perfect for growing acid-loving plants such as rhododendrons, azaleas, camellias, and blueberries. Other specific mixes include orchid potting mix and very free-draining potting mix for cacti and succulents.

When putting together color schemes for container plants, I think you should be influenced by your own personal tastes. Color has such an effect on mood that it's essential for our choices to make us happy. In my view, it's one of the most important areas to consider when planning your container garden.

CHOOSING COLORS

On my balcony, I focus on a select palette of colors, as lots of colors in a small space make it look too busy and small. If your garden leads off from a living space, include plant colors that match elements of the interior décor. For example, if I had purple cushions in a living room, I would choose purple plants like lavender or violets; if I had a picture on the wall with a splash of deep pink, then a pink achillea, for example, would look striking in a pot outside. Being aware of these color effects will help maintain a synergy between inside and outside.

Color and mood
I normally divide color schemes into four main groups. These are only guidelines, but I think they are a helpful starting point. When deciding on a color scheme, consider how you might create different moods.
Vibrant Bold, bright colors create a lively, energetic planting scheme. Opt for those plants with hot colors such as bright yellow daffodils and crimson red tulips in the spring, and yellow rudbeckias or golden achilleas, plus sizzling orange nasturtiums and crimson nicotianas in the summer months.
Ethereal Cool, soothing, and relaxing colors such as pale pinks, pale mauves, pale blues, and silvers will create a harmonious planting scheme.
Mysterious Choose plants with unusual colors such as black ophiopogons, deep purple hyacinths, and lime-green nicotianas.
Seductive Rich, evocative colors such as dark reddish-brown (chocolate cosmos), burnt orange (amaryllis), and deep blue (agapanthus, eryngiums, and muscari) can all be used to create sultry effects.

Putting colors together
Once you have chosen a palette of key colors, think about how you can combine them for different effects. At a basic level, planting schemes can be either a "hot" explosion of reds, oranges, and yellows or a "cool" display of soft colors such as pale pink, pale blue, and pale mauve. To create more sophisticated effects, consider the following approaches to combining color:
Complementary Colors that complement each other such as blue and white or purple and yellow will look brighter still when planted together.
Color scaling Use a range of colors such as purple, red and pink that are similar and, therefore, harmonizing. An attractive combination might include purple iris, soft pink roses, and deep pink alliums.
Tone on tone Use the same color, but vary the tones to create an understated effect. Try combining whites, creams and silvers or varying shades of purple and lilac.

The power of green
I take green as an absolute given in a planting scheme and build up the other colors accordingly. Remember, green is available in a range of shades, from the deep green of hollies to the greyish-green of sages. Plants with colorful foliage like heucheras and silver-leaved eryngiums can also play a role in your displays.

Ethereal

Ethereal

Ethereal

Ethereal

Vibrant

Vibrant

Vibrant

Vibrant

Mysterious

Mysterious

Mysterious

Mysterious

Seductive

Seductive

Seductive

Seductive

As soon as you've prepared your containers, it's time to plant them up. It really is a good idea to decide on the location for each container first before you plant them because you'll find larger ones very difficult to move once they are filled with potting mix.

PLANTING CONTAINERS

WHAT YOU NEED

Container

Drainage material

Potting mix
(suitable for the
type of planting)

Moisture-retaining
granules

Selection of plants

Slow-release,
general-purpose
fertilizer pellets

Perfect potting

From experience, I've found that it's best to plant containers in the early morning or late afternoon when it's a little cooler. I give the plants plenty of water and some suitable plant food when planting.

1 Put some drainage material over the holes and then fill the container one-third to two-thirds full with potting mix. Saturate the mix with water. You can also add moisture-retaining granules, which will absorb and gradually release water.

2 Carefully remove the plants from their pots, gently teasing the roots apart, and place them in the container. Make sure that the tops of the rootballs are below the rim of the pot. Avoid packing plants right up to the rim and arrange them in different ways until you find the composition you like best.

3 Fill in the gaps between the plants with more potting mix and firm down gently, leaving about 1in (2.5cm) at the top so that you can water the plants easily. Container-grown plants are under stress to produce flowers in a small space and quickly use up the nutrients in the potting mix. So, mix some fertilizer pellets into the top of the mix (according to the manufacturer's instructions) to release nutrients throughout the growing period.

4 Give the container a really good watering again. Remember to water daily in summer until water runs out of the drainage holes.

GIVE YOUR POTS A FINISHED LOOK Add a mulch of slate, gravel, pebbles, shells, stone chippings, moss, or sand to give your container a more finished look. These decorative mulches also stop water evaporating too quickly from the container in hot weather.

Container-grown plants are more prone to the effects of cold and drought, for example, than garden plants, but a regular maintenance routine, particularly during the growing season, will ensure your plants put on a spectacular show.

AFTERCARE

Watering
Regular watering is the most important task for any gardener, so remember to water your plants daily from late spring to early fall. You may even have to water twice a day in very hot weather. You can use either a watering can or a garden hose, if you have an outdoor faucet (tap). Look out for useful attachments that fit on a kitchen or bathroom faucet (tap) if you are happy to run the hose through an open window. Of course, installing an automatic irrigation system to drip water at set times into your containers is another solution if you find watering a real chore. Also available are self-watering containers and adjustable water reservoirs that turn ordinary pots into self-watering planters.

Feeding
After watering, feeding is another crucial aspect of container growing. The nutrients in soil-less potting mixes will last for a month or so, while those in soil-based potting mixes should last for around two months. After these time periods, you'll need to start watering in a diluted liquid general-purpose fertilizer (according to the manufacturer's instructions) every week or two. Feed during the growing season (i.e. from mid-spring to early fall) and not during the winter. You can also add some slow-release general-purpose fertilizer pellets on planting that will last the growing season. Note that there are specially formulated fertilizers for specific plants such as roses and tomatoes, which have a different balance of nutrients to promote better flowering or fruiting.

Repotting, top-dressing, and potting on
You may be using the same containers for a number of displays each year, once for spring bulbs and then again for summer bedding plants or seasonal crops. It's a good idea to replace the potting mix completely when

TAKING STEM CUTTINGS Propagate shrubs and herbaceous plants by taking stem tip cuttings. Take the cuttings from the tips of the plant's stems (a length of 4in/10cm is sufficient). Trim the cuttings just below a leaf node and remove all the side shoots and leaves, apart from two at the top. Dip the ends of the cuttings into hormone rooting powder and insert into a small pot of potting mix. Water well and cover with a plastic bag secured with an elastic band or the cut-off bottom of a plastic drinks bottle. Keep on a windowsill while your cuttings take root.

Dead-heading

Feeding

Watering

you replant each container. However, I suggest that you simply top-dress plants such as small trees and shrubs that you are growing permanently in a container instead of repotting them completely. To do this, remove about 2in (5cm) of the potting mix from the top of the container and replace it with new potting mix. Of course, if your plant has outgrown its pot, then you'll need to pot it on to a larger container.

Dead-heading

Try to get into the habit of removing spent flowers and old leaves regularly, a process known as dead-heading. Not only does this keep your container displays looking tidy and encourage further flowering, but it also helps reduce the prevalence of pests and diseases that can linger in dead flowers and leaves.

Winter protection

Permanent plants are vulnerable to severe frosts, so move any containers with long-term occupants to a sheltered position. You can buy special container protectors for really sensitive plants, which will help insulate them against the cold.

Pests and diseases

Various pests and diseases can be a problem for balcony gardeners in spite of their elevated position. Aphids and grey mold are both common problems,

while some pests and diseases will attack particular vegetables and fruits. For ornamental plants, try using a spray bottle (clearly labeled) with diluted insecticide or a diluted solution of water and dish-washing detergent to control aphids. Where possible, use organic pesticides, insecticides, and fungicides. In severe cases, you may have to dispose of the affected plant altogether. If you don't want to use any chemicals at all on flowers or crops, use organic methods of pest control such as companion planting: for example, try growing marigolds with tomatoes and borage with strawberries to deter particular pests.

Companion planting (marigolds with tomatoes)

Label new plants in spring

Prune early-flowering shrubs in summer

Plant spring bulbs in the fall

Enjoy winter-flowering bulbs

One of the **advantages** of container gardening in a small urban space is that you have only a relatively limited area to **maintain**. You don't want those all-important **seasonal** tasks to become a chore, so try to regard caring for your plants as a means of **relaxing** and **unwinding**.

SEASONAL CARE

Spring

You're bound to be very enthusiastic at this time of year as you start considering what you'd like to grow.

In early spring, start a winter tidy-up, inspecting containers for damage, preparing and cleaning them, and removing any dead leaves from plants.
Cut back the previous season's dead plant material.
Buy a selection of seeds and summer-flowering bulbs, and then sow or plant them in your choice of container.
Choose new bedding plants and start planting up containers when all danger of frost is over.
Clearly label any new plants, seeds, or bulbs.
Look at your permanent plantings and completely repot or top-dress them with new potting mix.
Start feeding and watering plants.

Summer

This is going to be your busiest season and you'll need to keep on top of watering and feeding routines. Now is also the time to enjoy your garden as it blooms.

Continue to plant up containers with new summer blooms (there will be a wide choice available at garden centers and nurseries).
Keep up a regular watering and feeding routine: water your plants daily (if not twice daily) in hot periods, and feed weekly or fortnightly.
Dead-head plants to promote further flushes of flowers.
Be vigilant in looking out for pests and diseases.
Trim or shear over box plants.
Lightly prune or cut back early-flowering shrubs such as camellias and viburnums.

Cut back yellowing leaves on spring-flowering bulbs.
Cut back rampant growth or plants that have "bolted."
Start eating vegetables and herbs, as well as edible flowers such as violas and zucchini (courgettes).
Consider which bulbs you'd like to have next spring.

Fall

As the gardening year starts to draw to a close, now is the time to enjoy the fall colors and to reflect on your container successes (and failures).

Plant up new containers with spring-flowering bulbs.
Pick the last of any vegetables from your containers.
Prune and cut back dead branches and twigs from trees and shrubs to get them ready for winter.
Remove spent annual plants from their containers.
Consider whether a permanent tree or shrub has outgrown its space. If it has, make plans to give it away to a friend with a larger outdoor space.

Winter

If you've planned ahead, you can enjoy the structure and colors of evergreen plants such as holly, bay, and box.

Cover precious plants with a container cover to provide some winter protection.
Check whether your plants need a little water at this time of year.
Spend some time dreaming of next year; look through gardening books and catalogs, and decide on the plants that you'd like to grow in the following season.
Have a well-earned rest!

Sky-high gardening can be exhilarating. As you tend to your plants, you will have amazing views of the urban landscape. Although this provides a wonderful backdrop for plants and garden features, you'll have to choose your plants with care and make design decisions that take the prevailing conditions into account.

DIFFICULT AREAS

Dealing with wind and sun

Although owning a garden in the sky throws up some excellent opportunities for inventive gardening, you will be creating a garden with a distinctive microclimate. This means that you'll have to be both practical and resourceful when choosing plants and planning the layout of the space. Here are some useful points to consider:

Anchor garden features Many balcony and roof gardens can inevitably get very windy and blustery, so you'll need to make sure that containers, pieces of furniture and hard-landscaping features (like pieces of trellis or screens) are well anchored in order to withstand gusts from strong winds.

Use drought-tolerant plants Being elevated means that plants on balcony and roof gardens quickly dry out, so opt for drought-tolerant plants that have adapted to the water loss (or desiccation) caused by wind and sun. These include plants with narrow leaves such as phormiums, cordylines, and grasses; small-leaved plants like cotoneasters and escallonias; grey-leaved plants such as French lavender, rosemary, and thyme; alpines; and, of course, cacti and succulents.

Create a windbreak If your garden space is particularly blustery, then include windbreak plants such as Camelia and Box to protect your garden from the worst of the wind. Other reliable shelter plants are *Viburnum tinus* and junipers.

Drought-resistant plants

Anchored garden feature

Sun-loving rosemary

Bamboo windbreak & shade-loving ivies and ferns

Choose miniature beauties Choosing dwarf varieties of spring- and summer-flowering bulbs that will tolerate exposed locations is also sensible.

Dealing with shade

Balcony and roof gardens can also be shady and overlooked. Indeed, the heavy shade cast by neighboring buildings, as well as overhanging balconies belonging to the apartments above, can limit the types of plant you can grow. Fortunately, there are ways to make the most of these difficult conditions, as follows:

Opt for shade-loving plants Shade-loving plants such as box and heucheras are low-maintenance and also provide a striking, architectural look. Shade-loving climbers such as ivy and climbing hydrangea are also great for beginners and need little maintenance.

Beware, though, if you have craggy bricks and mortar because they like to climb into every nook and cranny, and can cause structural damage.

Overhanging balconies Balconies belonging to the apartment above can cast a shadow over your balcony, making your container garden shady. Again, choose shade-loving plants if necessary and remember to pay close attention to watering, as the balcony above can cast a rain shadow.

Use decorative tricks Use clever design tricks to brighten up a dull, shady area. For example, you can paint walls white; hang mirrors to bounce light back into the space; and use pale-colored, reflective gravel mulches. This will make your garden lighter and also give your plants extra light.

Once you have **planned** and **designed** the main **features** of your balcony or roof garden, as well as planted up your **containers**, it's time to add those all-important finishing **touches** and **accessories**. This is always great **fun** and there is a wide range of **decorative** objects to **enhance** your urban retreat.

DECORATIVE ELEMENTS

The finishing touches on your balcony or roof terrace can make a real difference to how inviting the space is and therefore how much time you'll actually want to spend there. I look in more detail at using your urban retreat as a place for entertaining in chapter 5, but here are just a few suggestions for decorating and adding your own personal signature to your garden:

Floor surfaces Look very carefully at the style of your property and then choose a suitable surface for the roof garden. Decking and low-maintenance Astroturf are both popular choices, but you can also install colored flooring materials that have been specially designed for roof gardens. Always remember to consult a qualified architect or structural engineer before embarking on any major structural changes to your balcony or roof garden.

Mood lighting Turn your urban garden into an intimate and welcoming space so that you'll use it in the evenings by adding pretty tea-lights, large candles in hurricane lamps and colorful lanterns. Finishing touches like this will turn your garden into an extension of your home.

Furniture Use lightweight furniture such as a metal bistro table and a couple of chairs to create an al fresco dining area. Folding furniture is obviously the best choice for a small space and can be packed away easily for the winter.

Parasols If you have a very sunny roof space, then provide some shade with a parasol. These are now available in a great range of sizes and styles. Whatever you choose, make sure that it is firmly anchored or weighted down.

Cushions and throws Use decorative items such as vibrant cushions and casual throws to brighten up your space and make chairs and seating more comfortable and attractive. Why not include some large floor cushions, too?

Water features If you have the space, then a water feature such as a wooden barrel or old tin bath planted with miniature waterlilies and other marginal plants can be very restful. An outdoor electric socket means that you can also enjoy the soothing sound of trickling water with a simple wall fountain or bubble jet.

CREATE FOCAL POINTS Use key plants such as standard sweet bay trees or perhaps elegant holly lollipops planted in containers or even a striking piece of sculpture (figurative or abstract) in order to create a focal point on your roof garden or terrace.

CHAPTER 2

URBAN SPACES

Most urban living spaces tend to be rather small, as are the adjoining garden areas, that is if you are lucky enough to have one. Here, I have presented a selection of interesting themes and decorative approaches that you can draw on when creating your own urban outdoor escape, even if it is in the middle of a buzzing metropolis. With a little imagination, you too can design a highly personal outdoor room in which to sit back and relax.

If you live in a part of the city that is surrounded by high-rises and busy roads, noise, and pollution, creating an urban retreat will greatly enhance your quality of life. Even the smallest of balconies and roof gardens may be used to create a "green" sanctuary in which the modern city-dweller can escape all the hustle and bustle.

URBAN RETREAT

Although this garden is designed to be a green urban oasis, it also celebrates the city with its use of metals, color blocks, and defined lines. If you have the space, you can use this garden as an extension of your indoor living area, creating an outside "green room" that both expands and enhances your house or apartment. Using container planting also gives you the flexibility to move your garden around. So, if you're planning to alter your apartment inside, you can then reflect these changes outside as well and re-arrange your planters appropriately. For this urban retreat, I selected plants for their architectural qualities, as well as for their color-blocking effects by mixing strong and bright colors in the same color combinations to create fresh, modern, and dynamic looks. One of the key plants for this dramatic effect is achillea, which is available in a range of vibrant colors. You could also include screening plants such as laurels and golden bamboos (see pages 38–39) to enclose the garden, providing much-needed privacy and increasing the amount of soothing greenery.

WHAT TO PLANT

Grasses (such as miscanthus, pennisetum, and red fountain grass)

Architectural plants (such as cordylines, phormiums, and yuccas)

Color-blocking plants (such as achilleas, dahlias, echinacea, heuchera, and solidago)

Grasses and architectural plants

The urban garden often relies on strong planting to have an impact in an often space-restricted area. This clean-lined contemporary garden allows you as a designer to sculpt nature using different heights, colors, and textures. Architectural planting helps to create a clear shape and outline in this modern scheme. I think grasses and cordylines work particularly well together here, especially when sitting next to each other. The soft grasses serve to offset the sharp, hard lines of the cordylines. I like to place bold and elegant grasses at the back of an urban garden because they add good visual interest with their forms and foliage. There is a huge variety of colors and textures to choose from, so you really can experiment, particularly when you place them with small plants at the front. Cordylines often have quite dramatic foliage, so often mix well with other strong shapes and are very easy to care for. They are strong architecturally and make ideal container plants; there is no need to fill the container with many of them because they create such a bold statement.

Color blocking

A woodland of bluebells, a field of poppies, and a meadow spotted with daffodils—these swathes of vivid colors provide some of nature's prettiest vistas. This is color blocking at its most basic and beautiful. If you want to create an impact in your outdoor space, color blocking is a great way to achieve it. Simple, fluid lines combining harmonious colors easily create interest and drama. Picking different flowers and plants with the same colors achieves a strong aesthetic that works well in a small space. I approach color blocking in much the same way that a fashion stylist approaches putting together a "look." I keep to three simple rules: "Tone and Contrast," often using different tonal shades to create a vivid backdrop (think pink and silver, yellow, and green); "The Clash"— don't be afraid to clash colors for an exotic-looking mix (try red and pinks, black, and silver); and, finally, "The Power of Three", as I think three simple yet decisive colors are a great combination (consider purple, pink, and blue). Repetition and volume are also important, particularly when you're using bright, bold colors. Repeating the same intense color creates a stunning look and there are so many variations to choose from!

Achillea

Coneflower

Ornate candelabra

Funky period chair

Red fountain grass

Balloon flower

HOW TO DECORATE YOUR URBAN RETREAT Choose a

scheme that suits your urban space, perhaps opting for clean
lines that have a modern appeal. Also, consider how you will
use the space: for dining, add a table and chairs; for sitting
out, add a chair or recliner. A small side table will suffice
if you don't have very much room, as will lots of cushions and
throws on the floor for seating.

By virtue of their location, outdoor spaces in urban areas can often have unsightly views, features, or even simply a neighbor's window that you would prefer to block out. There is a wide selection of screening plants available for disguising these urban eyesores, although I prefer to use evergreen plants because they provide good camouflage all through the year.

SCREENING PLANTS

WHAT YOU NEED

Container trough, 32in (80cm) in length

Broken "crocks" or small stones over the drainage holes

Soil-based potting mix

2 laurel screening plants, 6ft (2m) in height

2 golden bamboo screening plants, 10ft (3m) in height

If you are planning to plant a screen to obscure an ugly view, then inevitably you will want it to establish quickly and easily. Here, I have used two particularly good concealing plants: golden bamboo and laurel, both of which act as a living screen even when they are very young and simply improve as they mature. Before planting, place some broken "crocks" (remember that "crocks" can be broken pieces of polystyrene plant trays) or small stones over the holes in the base of the trough to improve drainage, and use a soil-based potting mix because this will be a permanent planting feature.

Getting the conditions right

Laurels can cope with full sun or shade, which makes them ideal for growing on balconies and roof gardens. They are also drought-tolerant, which means that they do not require much watering (always a bonus for the busy city-dweller). Laurels grow quickly, making them the perfect choice if you are looking for a fast-growing screening plant.

Golden bamboo, with its distinctive golden canes, will grow in full sun or light shade, but make sure that you position the plant where it will be sheltered from prevailing winds. This is because bamboo can suffer from wind scorch. If your area is susceptible to high winds, then it may be better to use the laurel instead. Unlike laurel plants, golden bamboo does require lots of watering, but has the advantage of producing a delicate screen very quickly.

Care and maintenance

These screening plants are easy to maintain and don't require much day-to-day care. Both laurel and bamboo will survive with minimal attention, but there are a few things to bear in mind after planting. Although they are both great in containers, you may wish to increase the level of watering during dry spells, and give them a suitable plant feed occasionally, especially if the container has a lot of drainage holes.

Golden bamboo

Laurel

KEEP IT LOW If you have only a low area to screen, then try planting a pretty dwarf hydrangea in an old wooden crate, or some squirrel tail grass in tall pots. Although not evergreen, this annual or short-lived perennial grass has delicate, pink-tinged, pale green seedheads that swish in the breeze. The slightly smaller, soft green hare's tail is another equally delightful grass. These grasses will create an architectural look when planted en masse, as well as adding much-needed height and structure.

Dwarf hydrangea

Even the most enthusiastic balcony gardener may start with the best of intentions, but life can often get in the way and it is usually the garden that suffers first. For this reason, I've come up with some helpful suggestions for the time-poor (or simply lazy) gardener who yearns for a blossoming garden without too much effort on their part in terms of maintenance.

THE LAZY GARDEN

WHAT TO PLANT

Box plants

Drought-busting plants (such as cordylines and *Festuca glauca*)

Perennials (such as sea holly)

Succulents (such as sedums and sempervivums)

This garden, with its hot, lazy ambience, contains an array of waxy, succulent plants surrounded by whitewashed walls and accented by colorful furniture and accessories. For this laidback approach to gardening, I've opted primarily for plants and flowers that are drought-busters and don't need to be watered very often. These include succulents, plants that obligingly store water in their leaves, stems, and roots, and perennials, which can be planted in your garden and then live for many years, dying back each winter and growing back in the spring without needing to be planted again. However, although they love the sun, these plants will welcome a drink during a bout of hot weather. A good idea is to add a top-dressing such as some horticultural gravel to the planters in order to help reduce evaporation and cut down on the amount of watering required.

Box plants

Using box–a key plant for lazy gardeners

A useful plant for this style of garden is box, an evergreen shrub that looks attractive immediately and is fully hardy. Although box can be trained into a variety of formal shapes, including balls, cones, and pyramids, you can also buy ready-clipped box, giving instant gratification for the lazy gardener. Box plants have a long life and need only to be repotted every two to three years, thus cutting down on care and maintenance work. You'll also need to clip your box plants occasionally with some topiary shears or a pair of small, cordless electric shears.

19

SHORT-CUTS TO SUCCESS A good way to decide what to grow in this type of garden is to buy flowers and plants already in pots from your local garden center rather than trying to grow them from seed yourself. I tend to mostly buy ready-grown. By using potted flowers and plants, you'll have a good idea of what they;ll look like before you plant them.

Sempervivums

Sedums & Festuca glauca

Drought-loving succulent

Sea holly

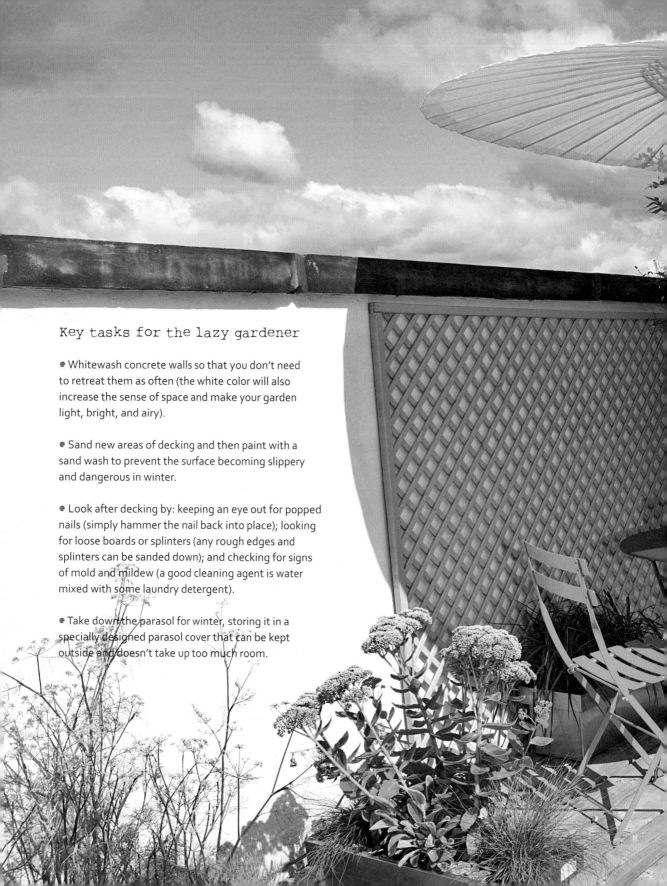

Key tasks for the lazy gardener

● Whitewash concrete walls so that you don't need to retreat them as often (the white color will also increase the sense of space and make your garden light, bright, and airy).

● Sand new areas of decking and then paint with a sand wash to prevent the surface becoming slippery and dangerous in winter.

● Look after decking by: keeping an eye out for popped nails (simply hammer the nail back into place); looking for loose boards or splinters (any rough edges and splinters can be sanded down); and checking for signs of mold and mildew (a good cleaning agent is water mixed with some laundry detergent).

● Take down the parasol for winter, storing it in a specially designed parasol cover that can be kept outside and doesn't take up too much room.

Evergreen window boxes can be planted with a classic mix of shrubs and foliage and finished off with an attractive, purple slate top-dressing. Plants such as these bring color to a drab winter landscape with their all-year greenness and vegetation—much needed for the urban gardener. The clean structural lines, as well as the strong focal points formed by the topiary box cone and dwarf pines, ensure that these year-round window boxes are perfect for a modern garden space.

EVERGREEN WINDOW BOXES

WHAT TO PLANT

Dwarf pines

Lavender

Pink dwarf rhododendrons

Red skimmia

Snowberry

Topiary box cone

Variegated ivy

White heather

An evergreen garden can provide a year-round base of evergreen foliage with seasonal changes being marked with displays of color from winter berries, spring bulbs, and summer blooms. There are plenty of bold evergreens to choose from, including box and pine, as well as silver-gray evergreens like lavender, which will all provide a strong foundation for your displays. Winter is when you are most likely to crave color in your garden, so introduce a selection of plants that will complement these evergreen plants. In the silver window box on the opposite page, I've used pretty dwarf pink rhododendrons with a box cone and lavender plants, while in the black window box, below, deep pink skimmia berries contrast boldly with dwarf pines, white heathers, and the gleaming white berries of a snowberry plant.

When you're designing an evergreen garden and deciding on the best place to put your window box, it's important to consider where the sun will fall. This is because east-facing walls will get a lot of morning sun, while west-facing walls will receive most of the sun in the afternoon and evening. Evergreen plants should be kept in a light spot in order to retain their color. Unfortunately, if they are placed in direct shade, they will lose their vibrancy and appeal.

White snowberry berries

Red skimmia, white heather, & dwarf pines

Variegated ivy

Gardening doesn't have to be a solitary activity. Easy-care and low-maintenance gardens can be created on the roof of an apartment block, providing an ideal spot for neighbors to gather together. A few plants here and there may improve the general appearance of a communal roof garden, but a small garden really will boost your shared outdoor living space.

SHARED SPACES

WHAT TO PLANT

Selection of perennials (such as hostas, heucheras, irises, bleeding heart, and peonies)

Selection of salad crops (such as different varieties of lettuce and cut-and-come-again salad leaves)

Edible herbs (such as basil, cilantro/coriander, dill, parsley, and arugula/rocket)

Selection of vegetables (such as potatoes, tomatoes, and zucchini/courgettes)

Communal gardens are often created as a response to a lack of green space in urban areas. They are also a great way of bringing neighbors and local communities closer together, something that is often difficult in cities. It's important to bear in mind everyone's preferences when planting the space. I would divide the garden into ornamental and productive areas, so that people have somewhere to relax and entertain, as well as an area in which to grow fresh produce.

Using Astroturf

If you and your neighbors have a balcony, or area of decking that needs refreshing, why not use some Astroturf to cover the surface? Nowadays, you can buy realistic-looking Astroturf (even including patches of dead grass). It is also great for children, as they can still have a safe patch of green to call their own. Your new "lawn" also won't require any watering, lawn fertilizers, or mowing and, on average, will last for 8–10 years.

Entertaining

After all your shared hard work in the garden, use your communal roof space for socializing—a great way to bond with your neighbors. If there is a generous budget, include a seating area with a couple of tables, which will always be welcome at communal barbecues and celebrations. Obviously, folding furniture is a good option for a shared garden where space may be at a premium at other times.

PERENNIALS For the ornamental garden, I've selected disease-resistant perennials that are tolerant of most growing conditions and fairly hardy. The majority of perennials are perfect for busy people, happily taking care of themselves without too much attention.

How to care for astroturf

● Most Astroturf companies recommend that you rake newly laid turf a number of times to make sure that the fibers stand up.

● Rake the turf during seasonal changes to remove fallen leaves, foliage, or other debris.

● Brush the turf regularly to prevent it compacting—simply brush it in the same direction.

● Remove any marks with a gentle detergent and some warm water. You can rely on rain to keep the turf clean (it drains away naturally, as does melting snow).

● Lightly mist the turf with a fine spray from a garden hose during dry spells.

Astroturf

Sweet basil

Mixed salad leaves

Flat-leaved parsley

Communal vegetable plots

I have always been a very keen advocate of "growing your own," and it's getting easier and easier to grow edible produce in small, urban outdoor spaces. Rather than gardening alone, however, many amateur gardeners are now joining forces with like-minded friends and neighbors in order to grow their own food together. What a wonderful way to foster a sense of community, eat healthily, reduce your carbon footprint, and save a little money at the same time. I think a communal garden is a wonderful way to grow vegetables, particularly if you are planning a community barbecue for the end of the summer.

For this reason, I've also included a small herb and vegetable plot in this rooftop garden to reflect the growing interest in home-grown produce. What could be better than to pick ingredients such as tomatoes or zucchini (courgettes) straight from a shared vegetable garden? Lettuce and other salad leaves are also relatively easy to grow and need to be picked regularly so that they don't set seed. They are then close to hand and easy to use whenever you or your neighbors need a quick, healthy meal at home.

You'll feel a real sense of pride when you serve and share food using ingredients like salad leaves and herbs sourced from your joint veggie patch.

Planting ideas for shared vegetable plots

● Zucchini (courgettes) are great for a shared space, spreading rapidly and looking after themselves with just a little watering. The flowers are also edible.

● Tomatoes are another crop that I recommend for a communal space. Good starting varieties are 'Gardener's Delight' (cherry tomato), 'Marzano' (plum), and 'Costoluto Fiorentino' (beefsteak).

● Companion plants work well with tomatoes, so why not plant some sweet basil with them? Not only will this keep away white fly, but you'll also have the ingredients for your favorite Mediterranean dishes.

For me, taking a trip to a country garden is the perfect opportunity to escape the urban sprawl and relax. But, like most people, I don't always have the time to leave the city for an afternoon when I need a moment of respite. What I've created here is a garden for city-dwellers that typifies the pleasure and leisure of an English country garden—a perfect place to unwind and read your newspaper on a lazy Sunday afternoon.

THE COUNTRY GARDEN

A summer afternoon spent in the countryside evokes thoughts of lush meadows, wildflowers, and beautiful woodlands. And with this project you can bring that same feeling to your own small outdoor space. I think it's a great addition to any garden in an urban sprawl, helping to provide a wonderful oasis. I find it just as relaxing to sit within my country garden as I do to gaze at it from indoors.

For the country-garden arrangement shown on the opposite page, I selected a classic, romantic blend of wistful shrubs and colorful flowers. I also used a wide range of different containers and plants of varying heights. It's easy to change the arrangement around to get different feels and views.

Key country plants

An English country garden is a combination of formal and informal planting. This garden takes its inspiration from the countryside and has been adapted for a small urban space. You can achieve a great deal with a few key containers, while the wildflowers, miniature roses, and attractive shrubs all help to create a wistful country look. These plants are easy to care for and, beyond regular watering, don't require too much maintenance. I've also selected some bold-colored foxgloves to draw the attention; they add a good dash of purple and blue. It's important, though, to make sure the soil is well drained, though, and the container placed in a sunny spot to start with. Focal points created by plants such as globe artichokes would also work well here. Anenomes are pretty country plants that grow well in containers, needing moist but well-drained soil. A lovely addition is the wildlife-attracting plants such as marigolds, lilacs, and sweet peas. For a green backdrop, consider including shade-loving ferns in the planting scheme.

WHAT TO PLANT

Here are some ideas for your English country garden:

Anemones

Azaleas

Catmint

Culinary herbs

Delphiniums

English lavender

Lollipop bay

Ferns

Foxgloves

Fuchsias

Globe artichokes

Hydrangeas

Lilacs

Lilies

Lupines

Marigolds

Miniature roses

Passionflower

Rosemary

Snapdragons

Spiraea

Sweet peas

Wisteria tree, potted

Delphiniums

Miniature rose

Lavender & azaleas

Decorating your rural idyll

The English country garden look is a nostalgic one, looking back to and evoking a bygone era of afternoon tea, bandstands, and watching cricket. For me, it represents the quintessential English landscape, casual and rustic, elegantly informal and charming. To enhance the country plants in this garden, I used muted or pastel shades for the walls, furniture, and planters and then added a variety of accessories, including both modern and rustic vintage finds. When selecting furniture, opt for bistro-style table sets, tables made from distressed wood such as oak, or pieces of painted furniture. You'll want to make your chairs more comfortable with cushions and throws, so choose fabrics with brightly colored, feminine patterns (such as chintz) and stripes, as well as natural fabrics like linen. You can also indulge yourself with the accessories. These decorative items might be a vintage wooden chair, a battered, old watering can, or a lovely floral cushion. Why not also include an outdoor thermometer or a water feature, whether this is a simple water bath or wall-mounted fountain.

How to enhance your country garden

● Welcome wildlife into your garden by adding a bird box or bird bath, which will give it a country feel.

● Use rustic and vintage garden furniture for added charm.

● Recreate a traditional English village feel by hanging up bunting and fabric lanterns.

● Use a wide variety of containers. I tend to opt for containers made from classic materials such as terracotta, aged zinc, beaten metal, or wicker.

Rosemary

If you're living in a city surrounded by high-rises and office buildings, you may feel bereft of **natural wildlife**—sometimes it can seem as if the only signs of it are city pigeons. There are ways to conquer this, however, by using the **plants** in your **window box** or on your balcony or roof-top garden to encourage **butterflies** and **bees** to visit your city home.

BUTTERFLY AND BEE WINDOW BOX

There is nothing more captivating than seeing a butterfly flit from flower to flower, and it is also important to encourage the butterfly population for environmental reasons. Over the years, many natural butterfly habitats have been lost due to urban spread and other human activities. By creating a butterfly garden, you are ensuring we can all enjoy watching them for years to come. Butterflies are also a great way to engage children in the garden and increase their interest in the outdoor world.

You can create an urban garden alive with pretty butterflies and pollinating bees by growing nectar-producing plants such as lavender, marigolds, and garlic chives. It is important to have flowers from mid- to late summer when most butterflies are at their most active. Butterfly bushes are the most popular flowers used by butterfly gardeners, and you can buy compact versions that can be grown in containers in confined spaces. With a little thought, your green space will soon be busy with visiting butterflies.

A garden alive with bees
If you wish to attract bees as well as butterflies, remember that different species of bee feed on different flowers, so try to include a good range of flowers for them. Bees especially seem to like lavender, and you'll often see lavender plants humming with bees in the summer. Although bees will happily set up home in secluded corners, you can also buy special bee boxes for attaching to a wall or even to a piece of trellis.

How to play host to a butterfly family
If you would like to welcome a family of butterflies, include some butterfly host plants such as sunflowers to provide a place on which the butterflies can lay their eggs, as well as a food source for the emerging caterpillars. Be prepared, though, for heavy munching on your host plants!

Onopordum acanthium

KEEPING BEES IN HIVES

Urban beekeeping is growing in popularity. Urban honey tends to have more flavor than country honey due to the wide variety of plants grown in cities. Recently, bees have been kept in Regents Park, London. As a result of floral diversity, the honey's taste, color, and texture change with the flowers. Also, because the honey contains traces of the local pollen (the allergen), it may prove a good remedy to try if you suffer from hayfever, as it helps to strengthen the immune system.

A window box placed by an often-open window brings a wonderful fragrance to your home. Summer breezes will carry in the soft scents of the flowers, plants, and herbs in the box. You can easily tailor a window box to your own tastes and include your favorite fragrances; this is natural aromatherapy at its best and simplest.

FRAGRANT WINDOW BOXES

WHAT TO PLANT

Alyssum

Eucalyptus

Gardenias

Herbs (such as mint, rosemary, and lemon thyme)

Jasmine

Lavender

Nasturtiums

Passionflower

Pelargoniums

Roses

Violas

Candles and incense may provide fragrance in the home, but they're no substitute for the heady scent of plants, flowers, and herbs. Scented plants offer endless scope for experimentation. You can, for example, create fragrant window boxes for different rooms in your home, such as a culinary herb window box near the kitchen, and a lavender-filled window box near a bedroom—the possibilities are limitless.

Choosing your scented plants

Fragrant plants that flourish in a window box include lavender, jasmine, gardenias, nasturtiums, and alyssum. They're all plants that grow well with other plants and are delightfully scented. Eucalyptus is a good companion plant, working as a contrast to the others in appearance and often enhancing other scents. Geraniums make a great centerpiece, as well as providing a focal point in a window box.

Herbs always grow well in window boxes and give off a fresh scent, particularly after summer rain. Many herbs produce a delicious scent when the leaves are rubbed between the fingers. Use herbs in your cooking and with care for their reputed medicinal properties to treat minor ailments.

Harnessing the power of fragrance

Many plants and flowers have scents with different properties that are closely associated with personal experiences and people. Lavender, for example, may remind you of a comforting relative or vacation in France; jasmine may evoke a favorite perfume; and rosemary might be one of your preferred cooking ingredients. You can also create a fragrant box for different therapeutic effects, whether this is lavender to aid relaxation, lemon thyme to invigorate you, or fresh mint to awaken both mind and spirit.

Violas & thyme

Passion flower & lavender

ENCOURAGING YOUNG CHILDREN Terrariums are a great way to encourage children to try gardening, providing them with their own little garden to care for and educating them about plants. They can pick woodland findings or plant and grow seeds in their very own glasshouse, creating a fantasy world by adding some painted pots and small toys. They will find it even more rewarding if they can watch their efforts grow from their bedrooms.

Terrarium gardens hark back to the **Victorian** era when indoor gardens housed in glass were very popular. **Many people grew these small gardens in large "Wardian cases"** at home. **Over the past few years,** terrariums **have made a comeback, as people look for** inventive **and** original **ways to grow plants in a protected environment.**

TERRARIUM GARDENS

WHAT TO PLANT

Under the large glass terrarium shown opposite I have placed small terracotta pots of variegated fittonia and nertera, but you might also like to try the following plants:

Dwarf hydrangeas

Ferns and mosses

Small cacti

Spring flowers (such as primroses and violets)

In the past, terrarium gardens were enclosed in Wardian cases, which look like small greenhouses with embellishments. However, you can create a terrarium with different receptacles. Cloches are popular, but modern-day interpretations could be on a smaller scale, including a glass cookie jar, a decorative vase, or even a cocktail glass. Keep the terrarium in a spot that receives indirect sunlight and doesn't fluctuate in temperature.

Plants that grow well in a terrarium and are easy to care for include ferns, cacti, mosses and a selection of houseplants. It is more interesting to choose plants in a range of different sizes, including tall, upright plants and smaller, creeping ones. You can grow your plants in individual terracotta pots, which you then keep under the glass case. However, many plants will thrive and grow completely encased in glass, seldom needing much care or attention from outside because they are situated in a sealed mini-greenhouse that recycles moisture as it evaporates and then condenses on the glass.

Planting a sealed terrarium

1 Before planting, clean the terrarium thoroughly to avoid a build-up of fungal diseases or algae, which will inevitably flourish in the enclosed environment.

Dwarf hydrangea

Primrose & violets

2 Don't forget to add a layer of drainage material such as pebbles or gravel, as well as some horticultural charcoal, to keep the potting mix fresh. Lightweight but moisture-retentive potting mixes make the best planting mediums.

3 Water your new plants well before planting and make sure that you give them enough space to grow.

4 Place moss or pebbles over the gaps in the planting to stop water evaporating and make your garden look attractive. Once established, a sealed terrarium will need very little watering to thrive.

The sound of water **rippling** and **splashing** over rocks or the **wildlife** that a pond attracts is a **lovely addition** to any garden. If you feel that you don't have enough space for a **water garden**, don't despair because there are many **opportunities** for creating an interesting, miniature water **feature** in even the tiniest of spaces.

WATER GARDENS

*Scirpus cernuus &
pale galingale*

Small water gardens are a lovely way to get really close to aquatic plants and enjoy their foliage and scents. If you think outside the box, there are many different ornamental containers suitable for a water garden. Simply think small and you can house a pond in a teacup, or in a dolly tub if you want a containerized water garden on a slightly larger scale. In short, anything that holds water can house a water garden.

Preparing your container
If there are holes in your container, plug them with corks to ensure that it's watertight. If you're using a wooden or porous container, it's best to line it first with a durable plastic liner. This prevents any toxins from oozing into the water. If you are using a clay container, apply a sealant to stop the water seeping through the clay. A layer of gravel at the top of the pot will also prevent the potting mix from spoiling the water clarity.

Choosing plants for your water garden
I would avoid putting too many plants in one container at first. Instead, gently build up your collection of water flowers using slender irises and colorful miniature waterlilies. Floating plants such as water lettuce or water hyacinth will look romantic and wistful against the sheen of the water. For a restless gardener, water gardens are perfect because you can move plants around easily and experiment with different colors and patterns.

*Water lettuce &
Scirpus cernuus*

WATCH OUT FOR FLIES Although it's delightful to have fresh water in your urban oasis, remember that water will attract flies. For this reason, I suggest siting your water garden in a corner of the roof garden, if at all possible to help prevent them coming into your house or apartment.

WHAT TO PLANT

You can grow only a limited selection of plants in a contained water garden, but there are still a few excellent aquatics to choose from, including:

Floating plants (such as water lettuce and water hyacinth)

Miniature waterlilies (e.g. 'Pygmaea Alba', 'Pygmaea Helvola', and 'Pygmaea Rubra')

Pale galingale

Scirpus cernuus

If you **yearn for the beach** in your cityscape, then this quick and easy container will provide all the elements of a **windswept landscape** without you having to head for the shore. You can use anything inspired by the beach, such as **shells** and pieces of **weathered driftwood,** to help you set the scene.

BEACH GARDEN IN A POT

WHAT YOU NEED

Large pot

Potting mix

3 small seashore plants (I have planted the blue-gray grass, *Festuca glauca*, as well as the cushion-like *Scleranthus biflorus* and *S. uniflorus*)

Fine sand (children's play sand is ideal)

Large shell

Coral

Growing up, I spent many summers on the coast and one of the things that I long for most on a hot summer's day in the city is the sense of calm I get when walking along a beach with a warm sea breeze and the sound of the ocean lapping at the shore. Admittedly, this container doesn't quite provide all those elements, but the sand and the distinctive plants that you find in an ocean landscape will help jog your memory and give you a feeling of serenity.

Here, I have used a deckchair and some other objects found on my travels, such as coral, large shells, and wood, to enhance that beach "feeling". This is a great way to transport yourself to the seashore, so, while you are on your travels, find things that will remind you of those special times and see if you can incorporate them into your beach garden at home.

I think this beach garden will bring the calm and serenity of a seashore retreat to your small urban space.

1 Fill the pot about three-quarters full with some potting mix.

2 Position the plants in the pot, teasing out the roots first, and then add more potting mix to within 2in (5cm) of the rim. Firm down the potting mix around the plants, and water thoroughly.

3 Carefully pour sand right to the top of the pot, and then place the shell and piece of coral in the spaces between the plants.

4 Set the pot in a sunny position near the deckchair ... and enjoy!

If you are without any outdoor space or even suitable window ledges for a window box, there are still ways to be creative with plants. In fact, front-door areas and entranceways are a fantastic opportunity to create an attractive container garden even in the most restricted of spaces.

FRONT-DOOR ARRANGEMENTS

WHAT TO PLANT

You can choose permanent shrub plantings, as well as seasonal container plants like spring and fall bulbs and summer annuals, to enhance your front-door area. Here are just a few suggestions:

In the dolly tub

Purple smoke bush

Variegated hebe

Dogwood (I have chosen *Cornus alba* 'Elegantissima')

On the wall ladder

Cyclamen

Dwarf hydrangea

Grasses

Sempervivums

In the terracotta planters

Lavender

Rosemary

Even a few pots can brighten up an entrance area and make it look more welcoming. If you are limited by space, then I would recommend having a wall ladder for pots. Using the vertical dimension in this way saves on space and yet visitors are still greeted by an array of plants and colors as they arrive. Herbs can also be grown by the front door, and their heady scents will greet guests. Both lavender and rosemary are great herb bushes for container planting and also easy to care for.

You can ring in the seasonal changes, too, by hanging a wreath on the front door at Christmas or by decorating the area with some Indian lanterns during the summer. Remember to opt for a style that reflects the interior décor of your home; for example, would metal or ceramic planters best enhance the inside of your home? For security reasons, I also suggest that accessories be kept to a minimum and if they don't weigh very much, then you might want to consider bolting them down.

If you would like to light up your front-door area, you'll find that small solar lanterns work well in pots. Alternatively, place small lights up the stairs to illuminate your entranceway and show off your flowers and plants.

ALL-IMPORTANT FIRST IMPRESSIONS

If you have unsightly meter boxes or unattractive trash cans outside your front door, then either paint them or disguise them with beautifully planted and well-positioned planters. I would recommend putting these containers on caster bases so that they can be easily moved around.

CHAPTER 3

CREATIVE RECYCLING

Balcony gardening doesn't need to be expensive and can also allow you to be very creative by using a variety of different recycled containers, from an old can to a wooden pallet. Creative recycling involves thinking outside the box and using what you have to hand to house your container garden. This is the wonder of container gardening: you can use anything to contain it. So, take inspiration from what's around you and enhance your outdoor space in a very individual manner.

Yellow chilli peppers

Eye-catching, Italian olive oil drums make **wonderful,** inexpensive, and **innovative** planters; they are **brightly** colored, **metallic,** and a great **addition** to any urban garden. I usually grow herbs in mine because they suit the drum size available and also go well with the **lovely packaging.**

OLIVE OIL DRUMS

Orange and red chilli peppers

Container planting can be a good opportunity to indulge your imagination. Instead of feeling limited by the usual selection of planters, you now have the perfect excuse to play around with unusual and recycled containers. For example, olive oil drums and other food receptacles, such as tomato cans, will prove a creative way in which to grow plants if you are constrained by space or budget. They are great for creating an Italian feel in your small garden, and what could be nicer than picking basil for your pasta sauce from your outside olive oil drum? You can get empty olive oil cans from Italian restaurants and delicatessens. My local pizza restaurant is excellent; I've been able to use their old oil drums, and they even keep some for me in the kitchen. If necessary, you can also buy a catering olive can and transfer the contents to a plastic container—please note that you must love olive oil because the drums are quite large!

Planting your olive oil drum
As with any unusual container, it's important to make drainage holes in the bottom of the olive oil drum first. The best way to make the holes is to use a thick, hard masonry nail and a hammer. It also helps to place a layer of polystyrene "crocks" or small rocks at the bottom of the drum to help the water drain away. Then, fill the drum with a nutrient-rich potting mix or commercial potting soil. For drums this size, I would suggest growing chilli peppers, radishes, basil, or parsley. I especially love growing chilli peppers because they make great gifts and you can tap into your chilli plant for an abundance of visits and parties. You can also grow a range of attractive flowering plants; simply match the color of the flowers to the colors of the drum.

WHAT YOU NEED

Olive oil drum

Polystyrene "crocks" or small stones

Potting mix

Herbs and vegetables (e.g. basil, chilli peppers, parsley, and radishes)

Brightly colored flowers (e.g. gaillardias)

ENSURE YOUR PLANTS DON'T DRY OUT As with any form of container gardening, it's essential to keep up a regular watering routine to ensure that your plants are not stressed by a lack of water. So, get into the habit of checking the potting mix in the oil drum frequently for dryness and also that the leaves of your plants aren't wilting.

When it comes to growing your own, herbs are a great place to start. They're easy to maintain and rewarding because you will see fast results. Housing them in a wooden wine crate sets off the colors of the herbs and is a stylish addition to your patio or balcony. In the summer months, I love to stand on my balcony and enjoy the different scents emanating from the herbs.

WINE CRATE HERB BOX

INGREDIENTS TO HAND There is something rather wonderful about combining the aesthetic with the practical, and with a herb garden you do just that. I used a variety of herbs with differing textures and hues to create this beautiful, scented window box. I love the fact that I can have delicious, flavorsome herbs close to hand to use in all my favorite recipes.

WHAT YOU NEED

Wooden wine crate

Polystyrene "crocks" or small stones

Potting mix

Chives

Golden marjoram

Lemon thyme

Mint

Rosemary

Salvia officinalis 'Tricolor' (purple and white variegated sage)

Silver thyme (such as *Thymus vulgaris* 'Silver Poesie')

This wonderful small garden can be created out of a reused wooden crate or any raised box so it is an economical as well as practical container. To grow herbs successfully, it is important to prepare your container properly. Most crates have slats on the base, giving you that all-important drainage. However, if your box doesn't, simply drill or puncture a few drainage holes (see page 17) at the base to allow for excess water to drain away. Herbs also prefer free-draining growing conditions, so it's a good idea to mix in some horticultural grit with the potting mix before planting in order to improve the drainage for your herbs. I would also recommend lining the box with some landscape material to prevent the potting mix from falling out.

Planting your herbs

When putting herbs into the box, follow an ordered pattern and create lines with planting to ensure the herbs have enough room to grow. When planting your herbs, work from the back to the front. In the herb box shown here I have planted:

Back row: Mint, rosemary, and golden marjoram
Middle: Chives
Front: Silver thyme, purple and variegated sage and lemon thyme
Added extras: You may also wish to include some violas to add color to your herb box; they are edible and look great when used in salads.

Where to position

Herbs tend to thrive in a lot of sun, so position your wine crate herb box in a sunny area. There are, however, some herbs such as chives and parsley that prefer partial shade; both of these herbs grow well in shade and cooler weather.

I have always enjoyed sourcing vintage containers such as this wooden fruit crate to use on my own balcony—they can be relied on to create a unique and individual look. Even if you don't live in a period property, vintage style will set off your plants well and is a good starting-point when setting up your garden.

VINTAGE CRATE SALAD BOX

WHAT YOU NEED

Vintage fruit crate

Polystyrene "crocks" or small stones

Potting mix

Landscape material or weed-control membrane

Butterhead lettuce seeds or plugs (try 'Tom Thumb' and 'All-Year-Round')

Loose-leaf lettuce seeds or plugs (try 'Salad Bowl Red')

Wild arugula (rocket) seeds or plugs

I have planted this delightful salad-leaf garden in a rustic vintage fruit crate, which calls to mind long, relaxed evenings of *al fresco* dining. Growing and picking salad leaves in the center of the city is very rewarding, and there is something satisfying about neatly arranging the plants in rows according to their various colors and textures. You'll also find the square-shaped container helpful when planting out the rows and ordering the seeds.

Wooden crates have slatted bottoms, so you'll need to line the base first with a piece of landscape material or weed-control membrane, available from good building suppliers. Lining the crate in this way will prevent the potting mix falling out, but allow excess water to drain away.

Planting your salad box

I have chosen a selection of salad leaves in different colors. Not only is this more decorative, but it will also provide you with a variety of delicious leaves for your plate. Plant up the box using seeds or plugs (small baby plants). Most lettuce varieties can be sown at any time between spring and summer. If you are growing your leaves from seed, then follow the instructions on the seed packet. Sow the seeds or plant the plugs in drills (rows) of alternating colors. Here, I have arranged the plants in five rows from left to right, as follows: 'Salad Bowl Red' lettuce; butterhead lettuce; wild arugula; butterhead lettuce; and 'Salad Bowl Red' lettuce.

Where to position

Placing salad plants in direct sunlight will cause bolting and leave you with a bitter-tasting crop, so it's best to position your crate in a spot that doesn't receive any strong midday sun.

CUT-AND-COME-AGAIN SALAD LEAVES If you sow the seeds yourself, you'll be able to create a cut-and-come-again salad box, which means that your leaves will grow back after cutting. Remember to sow small batches of seed every couple of weeks. Harvest your salad leaves by snipping them off with a pair of scissors rather than tearing them away by hand.

Alpine plants are usually found decorating rocky terrains and mountains in France and Switzerland; for me, they are a lovely reminder of school vacations when I was a child. These delicate plants have gentle pastel colors, and their different shades of green are a welcome addition to any small garden.

ALPINE-PLANTED METAL CRATE

WHAT YOU NEED

Industrial metal crate with drainage holes

Polystyrene "crocks" or small stones

Potting mix

Alpine plants (here I have used orange helianthemums and pink *Erodium* × *variabile* 'Roseum')

Washed white pebbles

Alpines grow well in confined spaces such as containers because they have small roots and won't grow too big. They are also hardy in adverse weather conditions, which will prove helpful if you are gardening on a windy balcony. Alpines will grow well all year round, ensuring you have a tiny, twelve-month garden, while alpines such as thyme will thrive en masse in a container, creating a deliciously scented display. There are a few factors to bear in mind when growing alpines, but you should be able to enjoy an attractive, long-lasting garden with only a little preparation.

Growing alpines in containers

To grow alpines in containers, choose the potting mix carefully. The most suitable potting mix for the average alpine plant is a porous one that is full of leafmold or is nutrient-rich. If the potting mix is heavy, then lighten it by adding plenty of gravel or coarse sand and, although controversial, peat moss. I would also suggest changing the potting mix once a year for pot-grown alpines. During winter, you don't need to water alpines, but your watering routine needs to start with the arrival of spring. This great little project will look attractive in any garden, large or small. It's also very easy to look after because the alpines are hardy. To achieve a similar alpine effect, simply pack stones around an alpine-planted pot in a metal gabion, or pebble-holder (these are used to stabilize coastlines, hillsides, or roadsides). Gabions create an effect of sleek modernity, which is effective combined with the natural serenity of stone.

1 Drill or puncture drainage holes in the base of the metal crate (see page 17) and add some polystyrene "crocks" or small stones.

2 Fill the crate three-quarters full with potting mix and arrange the plants until you are happy with the display. Then fill l the crate with more potting mix until it is within 4in (10cm) of the rim.

3 Finish off your planted alpine crate with a top-dressing of washed white pebbles.

Small campanula in a gabion

creative recycling

For the small-space gardener, **pots** and **planters** can go a long way. Planting recycled containers allows you to **display** and make a **feature** out of many different flowers and plants on your **balcony** or **roof-top** garden. In many ways, the **containers** are as aesthetically **important** as the flowers, vegetables, or fruit that you choose.

BIRDCAGE PLANTER

WHAT YOU NEED

Birdcage planter

Moss or coir matting

Potting mix

Campanulas

Trailing plants
(here I have chosen
to use ivy)

Although terracotta pots and planters are always a great starting point for a balcony or roof-top garden, it's nice to be adventurous and discover more interesting ways to house your plants. Looking for recycled and eclectic containers such as this vintage birdcage will make your small garden much more interesting and individual.

You can either display a few planted pots in your birdcage planter or plant up the birdcage itself. If you decide to plant up the birdcage, then you'll need to treat it rather like a hanging basket and line the base with some moss or coir matting to give it a finished look before filling it with potting mix and planting up.

Where to position
It is best to site your birdcage planter in a spot where it is easily accessible, so that you have no difficulties in watering the plants regularly. Also, try to make sure that it receives enough sunlight to keep your plants flourishing. You can either suspend the birdcage or stand it on a small bench. If you're going to hang your birdcage up, then remember to use some sturdy brackets to provide support.

Choosing the right plants
If you are going to suspend the birdcage, then choose flowers and plants that look their best when they are dangling down and you are looking up at them. I think a good starting point is to try planting spillers such as campanulas and verbenas that bloom continuously through the summer months, as well as trailers like ivy or even strawberries.

ENJOY YOUR BIRDCAGE INDOORS Instead of hanging your birdcage up, you could keep it indoors as a terrarium and opt for small plants that will not overtake the container. I would suggest plants such as asparagus fern, spike mosses, and succulent aloe varieties, which all grown very well in small, indoor environments.

If you're restricted in terms of space, but yearn for a spot of greenery, then a wall planter is an efficient way to add some plants without taking up too much room. Instead of growing plants conventionally, vertical planting allows you to grow upward and gives plenty of scope for creative planting ideas.

PALLET WALL PLANTER

"Green walls" are getting more and more popular, as people look for more eco-friendly ways to garden and utilize space. The world's largest green wall, known as the Bio-Lung, was unveiled at the World Expo 2005 in Japan. At 480ft (150m) long, 50ft (15m) high, and containing a total of 200,000 plants made up of 200 different species, it was a representation of how plants can act as the lungs of a city. Green walls help reduce pollution and rainwater run-off, as well as effectively insulating buildings and providing a habitat for wildlife.

Creating your own green wall
You can cover walls with a living green blanket, either by growing plants on lightweight structures or on ready-planted wall panels that include a water supply for keeping the plants hydrated and blossoming. There are also smaller modular systems available that can be used to grow vegetables and herbs, as long as they are well irrigated. Although you can buy vertical planters from specialty suppliers, it's easy to make your own using reclaimed materials such as this wooden pallet. You may want to stain or paint the pallet first, but remember that it won't then be suitable for growing edibles. I have planted heathers in beautiful shades of pink and purple in this pallet.

Stapling the landscaping material in place

WHAT YOU NEED

Good-quality wooden pallet (painting or staining optional)

Landscape material

Pair of scissors

Large stapler

2 large bags of potting mix

12 heather plants (using a mixture of green ericas and purple callunas)

1 First you will need to cover the bottom, back, and sides of the pallet with the landscape material. Lay out the material and wrap it across the back of the pallet from one side to the other. Do this twice so that you have a double layer. Cut away the excess side, but make sure that you leave a flap of material to cover over the bottom end, which will eventually become the base of the pallet.

2 Pull the material taut and staple the material to the back and sides of the pallet. Fold a seam along the edges facing the front to finish it off. Ensure that you leave the top of the pallet open because you will want to plant up this space.

3 Lay the pallet on the ground and fill the opening at the top with potting mix. Plant up this section first by sliding in the heathers and packing them in very tightly.

4 Fill in the gaps between all the other slats with more potting mix, leaving enough room for the heather plants. Smooth out the potting mix ready for planting.

5 Plant the heathers tightly in the gaps between the slats, making sure you completely cover every opening.

6 Water thoroughly and leave for two weeks so that the plants root well and will be held securely. Once the plants have taken root, lean the planter against a wall.

Where to position

Think carefully about the right location for your planter by making sure that it will receive enough sun and not be disturbed by too much wind. Finally, and perhaps most importantly, check that you can reach the planter easily for feeding and watering purposes, and then remember to water it regularly and evenly.

Other planting ideas

Planting in the vertical dimension provides a great opportunity to grow trailing plants such as ferns and ivies, as well as drought-tolerant succulents like sedums and sempervivums. You may also wish to grow herbs such as thyme, oregano, and marjoram in the planter.

CHAPTER 4

ALL THINGS EDIBLE

From seed to plate... There really is nothing better than the novelty of seeing a small seedling transform into a lush edible plant. You will gain a real sense of achievement from growing your own produce, whether it's freshly picked herbs or some handpicked tomatoes. You also have the added benefit of being able to flavor your favorite dishes with fresh ingredients. Even in the smallest of spaces, you can easily achieve a little piece of the good life.

I'm a big advocate of home-grown vegetables, fruit, and herbs. I think that being able to grow crops at home in different containers is both great fun and hugely satisfying. From your window you can simply reach out and pick basil for pasta sauces, mint for cocktails, and tomatoes for salads.

GROWING CROPS IN POTS

Many people feel daunted by the thought of growing their own produce. I often convince people of the pleasures of home-growing by explaining the money to be saved. For example, instead of heading to the shops and spending money on ready-made salad bags that rarely last more than a few days, you can harvest your own leaves at home with cut-and-come-again crops.

When growing produce at home in a small space, choose vegetables that won't grow too big and are also

about your location. Ask yourself: Is my garden space in the shade? How much sun does it receive? Is it a windy spot? Based on your answers, choose vegetables that are best suited to your growing conditions. For example, salad greens flourish when shaded by bigger plants; tomatoes grow well in a sunny position and with marigolds planted beside them (the odor helps deter insect pests); and all container vegetables will thrive with a side dressing of potting mix once a month, along with weekly fertilizer. Most vegetables like four to six hours of sun daily, nutrient-rich potting mix, and good watering routines, so always bear these essentials in mind.

Successful crops

The crops in this section are just a few of the main edible plants that can be grown in containers or window boxes on a roof or balcony. It is by no means intended to be an exhaustive list, but it should get you off to a flying start.

The chart opposite is a guide to when to sow your seeds and harvest your crops. Do also be guided by the information on the seed packet instructions. Bear in mind the effect of your local growing conditions when transplanting tender plants if you have raised them indoors or under glass. Tender plants such as eggplants, chilli peppers, tomatoes, and cucumber, as well as herbs such as sage, basil, and thyme, will need to be gradually hardened off and accustomed to outdoor growing conditions before being transported to their final containers. To do this, use a cloche, bell jar, or some horticultural fleece. Remove the covering during the day and replace at night for a few weeks before planting. Plant once all the danger of frost has passed.

Make sure you'll use what you grow! Zucchini (courgettes), for example, can produce abundant crops, so be prepared to eat or store large amounts.

Seed	Where to grow	When to sow	When to harvest
BASIL	Windowsill	Late winter to mid-spring	Late spring to mid-fall
BELL PEPPERS	Indoors under glass	Early to mid-spring	Mid-summer to early fall
CARROTS	Directly in pot	From mid-spring	Late spring to late fall
CHERVIL	Windowsill	Early spring to late summer	Late spring to late fall
CHILLI PEPPER	Windowsill/indoors under glass	Mid-winter to late spring	Mid- to late summer
CHIVES	Directly in pot	Early spring to early summer	Mid-summer to late fall
CILANTRO (coriander)	Directly in pot/windowsill	Early spring to late summer	Late spring to mid-fall
CUCUMBER	Indoors under glass	Early spring to early summer	Mid-summer to early fall
DILL	Windowsill/directly in pot	Early spring to mid-summer	Mid-summer to early fall
EGGPLANT (aubergine)	Indoors under glass	Early to mid-spring	Mid-summer to mid-fall
MARJORAM	Indoors under glass	Early to late summer	Late summer to early winter
MINT	Directly in pot	Late winter to mid-summer	Late summer to early fall
OREGANO	Indoors under glass	Early spring to early summer	Early summer to mid-fall
PARSLEY	Indoors under glass/direct/windowsill	Early spring to mid-summer	Late spring to late fall
PEAS	Directly in pot	Early spring to early fall	Early to late summer
RADISH	Directly in pot	Late winter to late summer	Mid-spring to mid-fall
ROSEMARY	Indoors under glass	Early to late spring	Mid-summer to mid-fall
SAGE	Indoors under glass	Early to late spring	Early summer to mid-fall
SALAD LEAVES	Directly in pot/windowsill	Early spring to late summer	Late spring to mid-fall
SCALLIONS (spring onions)	Directly in pot	Early spring to mid-summer	Early summer to mid-fall
SORREL	Directly in pot	Early spring to late summer	Late spring to late fall
THYME	Indoors under glass	Early to mid-spring	Early summer to mid-fall
TOMATO	Indoors under glass	Early to mid-spring	Mid-summer to late fall
ZUCCHINI (courgettes)	Indoors under glass/direct	Late spring to early summer	Early summer to early fall

If you're limited to just one container in a confined space, then you can still grow and enjoy enough produce for a wealth of summer dishes. If you plant with favorite recipes in mind, you'll be stocked up with useful ingredients that you can cook with regularly. This is sustainable growing at its best and can be achieved in just one window box.

Tomato plant

MEDITERRANEAN PLANTER

WHAT YOU NEED

Wooden window box

Polystyrene "crocks" or small stones

Potting mix

Horticultural grit

Plant feed

Tomato plant in a large pot

In the window box, I included a chilli pepper plant and a selection of culinary herbs, as follows:

Bush basil

Curry plant

Golden thyme

Marjoram ('Acorn Bank')

Oregano

Purple basil ('Dark Opal')

For a summery Mediterranean container such as this, I've chosen ingredients that can be used in three of my favorite recipes: baked herb tomatoes, spiced herb tomato chutney, and a Bloody Mary cocktail. The recipe for this delicious chutney is given on the opposite page. You can, of course, also use the ingredients to make a classic tomato and basil sauce to serve with your favorite pasta. Using a rustic-looking wooden window box as the container, I planted oregano, chilli peppers, marjoram, curry plant (which is used to flavor mayonnaise in Mediterranean cooking), and golden thyme, as well as two types of pungent basil. I also planted a tomato plant in a separate pot, as this is such a staple of Mediterranean cooking. For more guidance on growing fresh tomatoes at home, see pages 104–106. Even if you are new to growing your own produce, you should find that all of these plants are easy-to-grow and will keep you well stocked with useful ingredients.

Planting your window box

It's a good idea to start off your plants from seedlings grown in small pots, ideally indoors or under glass, and to keep the potting mix moist and warm. You can then transfer more mature plants to the window box outside once any danger of frost has passed. Make sure that there are adequate drainage holes in the bottom of the box to keep the potting mix healthy and remember to allow for enough growing space between the plants when planting. It's also a good idea to incorporate a little horticultural grit with the potting mix to create the free-draining growing conditions that herbs prefer.

Where to position

I recommend placing your window box in a spot that receives between six and eight hours of sun a day. After a few months, you will have enough produce to include in a host of mouth-watering dishes.

Serves: 5-6
Preparation time:
10 minutes
Cooking time: 10-14
minutes

Ingredients
3 tbsp olive oil
6 tomatoes, chopped
1½ shallots, chopped
1 garlic clove,
  finely crushed
½ red chilli pepper,
  chopped (optional)
¼ tsp paprika
1 tbsp finely
  shredded fresh
  basil
1 tbsp chopped
  fresh oregano
3 tsp brown sugar
3 tbsp balsamic
  vinegar

This delicious chutney is a
great accompaniment to cheese.

EASY SPICED HERB TOMATO CHUTNEY

1 Heat the olive oil in a pan. Add the
tomatoes, shallots, garlic, chilli pepper
(if using), paprika, basil, and oregano to
the pan and cook for 5–8 minutes or until
softened.
2 Add the sugar and vinegar, cook for a
further 5–6 minutes, or until the chutney
has caramelized slightly. Serve with
cheese and crusty bread.

Spiced herb tomato chutney

If you want to create a window box that will supply you with useful ingredients, why not grow a selection of culinary herbs to accompany some of your favorite meat and poultry dishes? For this window box, I've selected herbs that complement chicken and, of course, also work well in a range of other poultry dishes.

HERB WINDOW BOX FOR CHICKEN

WHAT YOU NEED

Black window box

Polystyrene "crocks" or small stone

Potting mix

Horticultural grit

Seaweed extract fertilizer

Blackcurrant sage

Compact marjoram

French tarragon

Golden thyme

Hamburg root parsley

Purple sage

This is a great culinary window box, and you'll be able to reach out and pick instant ingredients and garnishes for your various recipes. So many herbs can be used to enhance the flavor of different meats and poultry. Indeed, several of these herbs are versatile enough to be used in a range of delicious dishes. You may wish to design a bespoke window box with a specific meat in mind, so think about which meats you like to cook and what you enjoy as a flavoring.

For this window box, I have chosen a selection of herbs that go beautifully with chicken. It includes some unusual herbs such as blackcurrant sage and Hambury root parsley. All of the herbs used here can be planted together and aren't particularly invasive. They are also perennials, which means that they will last for a few years in the same window box. If you can't bring the window box indoors during the winter months, then use a cover to protect it against the frost. I mixed a few handfuls of horticultural grit into the potting mix before planting because herbs prefer well-drained growing conditions. You'll need to feed the herbs occasionally with some seaweed extract fertilizer, and remember to cut them back after they have flowered.

Sage

MATCH THE HERB TO THE MEAT I think the following herbs make good accompaniments to plenty of meat dishes and will all be great plants for a flavorsome and attractive window box. Personally, I think sage, sweet marjoram, summer savory, thyme, and tarragon are also good choices for poultry meats, while rosemary, star anise, chives, basil, and sweet marjoram are perfect for pork dishes. If you prefer beef, I would opt for summer savory, thyme, cilantro (coriander), sweet marjoram, and basil and, finally, garlic, rosemary, dill, mint, and summer savory for lamb.

You can't beat a simple roast chicken, and this flavorsome recipe is a great choice for Sunday lunch. I love to serve my roast chicken with olive-oil mash, honey-glazed carrots, and some steamed Savoy cabbage.

HERB-ROASTED BUTTER CHICKEN

1 Preheat the oven to 375°F/190°C/gas mark 5. In a bowl, mix together the butter, the rind and juice of one of the lemons, the herbs, garlic, and seasoning.
2 Gently loosen the chicken skin over the breast and legs, push in the butter mixture, and smooth it out evenly from the outside. Cut the other lemon in half and push it into the cavity of the bird.
3 Season the skin and place the chicken in the oven for around 1 hour and 20 minutes, basting the chicken occasionally with the buttery juices in the pan.
4 Remove the chicken from the oven to a plate and allow it to rest for 15 minutes before carving.

Serves: 4-6
Preparation time: 10 minutes
Cooking time: 1 hour and 20 minutes

Ingredients
6oz (175g) unsalted butter
2 lemons
2 tbsp chopped fresh tarragon
4 tbsp chopped fresh flat-leaved parsley
1 tbsp chopped fresh rosemary
1 tsp chopped fresh lemon thyme
1 garlic clove, peeled and chopped
sea salt and freshly ground black pepper
3lb 5oz (1.5kg) chicken

A **simple** fish dish cooked with herbs is a piece of **classic** cuisine. I have always loved picking up these **wonderful** herb selections for **fish** when on holiday in France. However, if you plant this **herbal** box yourself, there is no need to go so far afield and you'll be able to enjoy **fresh** herbs in your cooking whenever you wish!

HERB WINDOW BOX FOR FISH

WHAT YOU NEED

Metal window box
(this one is made
from aged zinc)

Polystyrene
"crocks" or small
stone

Potting mix

Horticultural grit

A selection of herbs
suitable for cooking
with fish (basil
mint, bronze fennel,
curly-leaved
parsley, dill,
English mace, lemon
thyme, orange-
scented thyme,
sage, and
sorrel)

For this window box, I have selected herbs that are often used in fish dishes, as well as a few other planting companions. The herbs are basil, bronze fennel, curly-leaved parsley, dill, English mace, lemon thyme, orange-scented thyme, and sorrel. It's best to plant your herbs from late spring to mid-fall, and, once the window box is blooming, you can enjoy the produce all year. Remember to mix in a little horticultural grit to the potting mix because herbs enjoy free-draining conditions.

Looking after your herbs

To maintain the herbs in this box, it's important to prune any faded stems to keep the plants compact. I also suggest that you pick the evergreen herbs from the top instead of the side to promote new growth. It's a good rule of thumb to feed the window box regularly with seaweed extract in order to encourage leaf production and help to maintain sweet and succulent plants. Neither parsley nor sorrel enjoy being in direct sun, so try to place the window box in partial shade.

INGREDIENTS FOR EVERY DAY The selection
of herbs in this window box sets off so many fish
dishes perfectly, including dill and salmon,
thyme and wild trout. I especially enjoy cooking
with fresh sorrel leaves and have found that their
sharp, lemony flavor can be used with dill and crème
fraîche or sour cream to make a wonderful sauce for
cold fish such as salmon.

Herb salmon & couscous parcels

Here is just one of the many recipes for fish with herbs that I enjoy cooking at home:

HERB SALMON AND COUSCOUS PARCELS

1 Put the couscous in a bowl and stir in the stock and oil. Cover with plastic wrap, leave to stand for 10 minutes, and then uncover and fluff up with a fork.
2 Keeping back some herbs, add the remainder of the ingredients (apart from the salmon, lemon, and seasoning) to the couscous. Season to taste.
3 Preheat the oven to 400°F/200°C/gas 6. Cut out four large sheets of non-stick parchment paper and divide the couscous mix between them. Sit each salmon fillet on the couscous, top with the remaining herbs, and season to taste. Fold the paper over and twist the edges to seal.
4 Place the parcels on a baking sheet and bake for 15 minutes or until the fish feels firm. Serve in the paper with a squeeze of lemon.

Serves: 4
Preparation time: 10 minutes
Cooking time: 30 minutes

Ingredients
4oz (110g) pack lemon and garlic couscous
   (available from most supermarkets)
1 cup (250ml) hot vegetable stock
1 tbsp olive oil
handful of chopped fresh herbs
   (such as basil, mint, orange-scented thyme
   and parsley)
4 scallions (spring onions), thinly sliced
4 sun-blush or sundried tomatoes, chopped
2 salmon fillets, weighing approx.
   6oz (175g) each
1 lemon
salt and freshly ground black pepper

If you're a **foodie** and enjoy spending time trying out **recipes** in the kitchen, why not plant up some containers to provide specific **ingredients** for your **favorite** dishes? Thai curries use lots of different **herbs** that can be easily **grown** in pots and **planters** ready to be picked for cooking.

CURRY WINDOW BOX

WHAT YOU NEED

Window box

Polystyrene "crocks" or small stones

Potting mix

A selection of herbs suitable for Thai curries (dwarf 'Apache' chilli pepper, cilantro, garlic, holy basil, kaffir lime and lemon grass)

This aromatic window box is planted with some of the most common ingredients in Thai curries. All of these Thai herbs and spices are simple to grow at home. Here, I've put together some helpful advice on growing each of these ingredients:

Cilantro (coriander) is an annual herb, which is best grown from seed sown directly in the potting mix. It's quite a sensitive plant and won't appreciate being moved around too much. The leaves can be harvested as soon as the plant is big and robust enough to cope.

Chilli peppers are easy to grow in most climates and similar to tomatoes in that they grow well in pots. The chillies used in Thai cooking are known as "bird's-eye chillies" and can be bought from most garden centers; often, the cooler the weather, the milder the chillies will be. Keep picking in order to let new chillies come through.

Garlic and shallots are alliums that like growing in a mixed climate. It's said that you should plant them on the shortest day of the year to harvest them on the longest day.

Ginger is best grown either indoors or in a sunny spot. To grow your own ginger, simply plant the "rhizome" (the root ginger that you buy from the store) in a pot. It needs regular watering and should be brought indoors in winter.

Holy basil Although often used in salads, I have found that holy, or sacred, basil tastes delicious in Thai curries. Like many herbs, it enjoys full sun and free-draining growing conditions, so add some horticultural grit to the potting mix as well. The leaves bruise easily, so take care when harvesting.

Kaffir lime trees can be bought as a standard tree or a starter one. You can use the leaves in Thai green curries. If you also want fragrant, zesty fruit, then choose a mature tree and place it in a sunny, sheltered spot in the ground.

Lemon grass is often an expensive ingredient to buy and rarely has the same taste as fresh lemon grass, which you'll find a lot more intense and lemony. Instead, I would suggest buying a few nursery plants and rooting them in well-watered potting mix in a sunny spot. You'll have to move them indoors when it gets colder, but they can be placed on a windowsill if you have limited space.

Once your Thai garden is ready to harvest, you can combine all the tasty ingredients to make your own Thai curry using eggplant (aubergine):

EGGPLANT THAI CURRY

1 Put the garlic, chilli peppers, ginger, lemon grass, turmeric, and cumin into a food-processor, blitz to a paste, and set aside.

2 Heat the olive oil in a frying pan, add the eggplant, cook until brown, and remove from the pan.

3 Cook the paste, sugar, and shallots for a few minutes and then return the eggplant to the pan. Add the fish sauce, coconut milk, kaffir leaves, and stock, and bring the liquid to a boil.

4 Gently simmer for about 15 minutes or until the eggplant is tender.

5 Season to taste and sprinkle the cilantro and holy basil over the top.

6 Serve with steamed sticky or jasmine rice.

Serves: 4
Preparation time: 20 minutes
Cooking time: 15 minutes

Ingredients
6 garlic cloves, roughly chopped
5 red chilli peppers, deseeded and chopped
1¾ in (4cm) piece of fresh ginger, chopped
2 lemon grass stalks, chopped
2 tbsp ground turmeric
½ tbsp cumin seeds
1 tbsp olive oil
2–3 eggplants, cut into
   2in (5cm) cubes (approx. 1lb 4oz/600g)
1 tbsp sugar
6 shallots, finely chopped
1 tbsp Thai fish sauce
1 x 14oz (400g) can coconut milk
2 kaffir lime leaves
1½ cups (375ml) vegetable stock
salt to taste
a handful of roughly chopped fresh cilantro
   and holy basil

Herbs have been used for centuries across the world, with people utilizing their unique and particular properties for herbal remedies to alleviate various medical conditions and upsets. They're not simple plants by any means and formed the foundations of modern medicine.

MEDICINAL HERBS

Before you start to use herbs for specific conditions, it's important to consult a doctor or qualified herbalist first so as to be completely sure of their effects. Once you're confident of these and you're sure of how to use the herbs, then you can start making the most of their therapeutic benefits.

Herbs are mostly hardy plants that will survive throughout the year with a little love from their owner, meaning that you can use them for home-made remedies as and when required. There are several herbs that can be grown in your urban outdoor space that will prove effective and easy-to-use remedies. For example, the ones that are suggested here include chamomile flowers to aid sleep, dill seed to help calm griping pains, peppermint leaves for improving digestion, and lemon balm to relieve tiredness and headaches.

Growing your own tea

Green, black, and white teas all come from the same plant, *Camellia sinensis*. It is really easy to make your own pot of fresh tea using this hardy plant, which will grow well on a balcony or roof garden. To make your own tea, you'll need about five to seven tea leaves per teapot. Just follow these simple steps:

1 Gently wash the leaves by running cold water over them through a sieve. Boil the kettle and put your tea leaves in the teapot.

2 Pour a little water into the teapot and then swirl the leaves around for ten seconds before filling the teapot with more boiling water.

3 Allow the tea to sit (brew) for about ten minutes and then pour yourself a refreshing cup of tea. You can reuse the leaves up to three times.

Making herbal tea

An easy way to exploit the medicinal properties of herbs is to make a tisane, or herbal tea, which can be a beneficial addition to your daily diet. To make one cup of herbal tea (use herbs such as chamomile, lemon balm, peppermint, rose petals, violets, and lavender) pick five fresh leaves or a sprig (depending on the herb). You can also use two teaspoons of dried herbs or one teaspoon of the seed. I usually place the herbs on a clean piece of kitchen paper and lightly crush them first. Then, add the herbs to a cup or teapot (if you are making more than one cup), pour over some slightly cooled boiled water, and cover. It's important to cover the cup to stop the beneficial essential oils evaporating with the steam. If necessary, strain the tea and sweeten with honey to taste.

Herbal tea

THE POWER OF ALOE VERA Aloe vera is a succulent plant that has the most amazing healing powers in its leaves. If you have a blister or sunburn or have been stung by an insect, simply break off one of the leaves and squeeze the juice over the affected area. You should find that this helps soothe and relieve any irritation. What could be nicer than having your own natural medicine cabinet close by?

One of my **favorite** window boxes is the cocktail-themed box, which makes a **wonderful** addition to any social butterfly's balcony. For these **recipes,** I simply selected a collection of **plants** used in my favorite **cocktails,** but you can **mix** and **match** as you wish.

COCKTAIL WINDOW BOX

WHAT YOU NEED

Zinc window box

Polystyrene "crocks" or small stones

Potting mix

Plant feed

Mint plants(I have used a couple of varieties for color: garden mint and red-stemmed apple mint)

Mini kumquat tree

Strawberry plants

This zinc window box is fresh and modern, making it perfect for the contemporary home. When in bloom it will look very colorful because it is planted with kumquats and strawberries. Sometimes strawberries will grow downwards, so I try to make sure there's plenty of room underneath the box. Buy strawberry plants early in the year so that they have time to fruit. I love looking at the kumquats in the center of the box, as they are particularly bright and vibrant. You need to get used to the taste of kumquat. Although often sour at first, the whole fruit can be eaten at once—peel included! Some kumquats may even ripen during the winter months, if kept inside.

Looking after your window box

Kumquats are the most frost-hardy of the citrus plants, but still need sun or at least partial sun. They also need to be brought inside when the weather cools. Feed with plant feed every couple of weeks to guarantee a good crop. Don't overwater the box, as waterlogged soil will cause the fruits to become diseased and the plants to rot. Fruit-bearing window boxes should also be sheltered from the wind. Pick the mint regularly, as it grows rapidly and can overtake a container. It is a good idea to keep the mint plant in its original plastic pot when planting up your box because it can be so invasive.

with your own fresh fruits...

PIMMS

1 cup (250ml) Pimms
4 cups (1 liter) lemonade
3 kumquats, sliced in half
3 strawberries, sliced
half cucumber, chopped
handful of fresh mint leaves

Mix all the ingredients together in a large pitcher.
Serve with ice or chilled.

a tangy spin on the classic...

KUMQUAT-GINGER CAIPIRINHA

5 kumquats, sliced
1 tsp chopped fresh ginger
1½-2 tbsp superfine (caster) sugar
¼ cup (ml) cachaca
slice of kumquat to garnish
sprig of mint to garnish

Place the kumquats, ginger, and sugar into an old-
fashioned glass and muddle well. Fill the glass with ice,
then add the cachaca. Stir well. Garnish with a slice of
kumquat and a sprig of mint.

SUMMER FUN Relaxing on your balcony or
roof terrace with a tasty cocktail in your hand
is a great way to spend a summer evening. This
window box contains all the ingredients to
embellish numerous cocktails, from Pimms and
Caipirinhas to mojitos and daiquiris. Using
mint, strawberries, and kumquats as your base,
you have the definitive party container! With
a favorite cocktail in your hand, I'm sure
you'll enjoy this window box as much as I do.

Herbs make both **decorative** and useful additions to an urban **kitchen** garden. They are **easy** to care for, provide **bushy** crops, and look very **attractive** in situ. You can have daily supplies of **herbs** to use as **garnishes** and cooking **ingredients**, and a few leaves will go a long way in your **recipes**.

HERBS

Growing herbs in containers is very rewarding for the small-space gardener. You can easily plant and grow six or seven different varieties of herb in various containers on your balcony or roof garden. Different herbs look great together and I don't think that you should be afraid of planting particular herbs in one container purely for aesthetic rather than culinary reasons. For example, you can combine purple plants with bright green ones, as well as mix different scents. I cannot think of a nicer fragrance than that of fresh mint, rosemary, or thyme after a summer rain.

Growing your herb garden

Most herbs are easy to grow in containers: choose from old wine crates, olive oil cans, hanging baskets, and window boxes, for example. Whatever containers you use, make sure they have adequate drainage holes.

Herbs can be grown from seed or bought as young plants and then transferred to your chosen containers. Once you've planted up the containers, choose a spot that receives plenty of sun. Be sure to keep an eye on your herb garden and ensure it receives enough water; you may need to move the pots around during particularly hot spells to stop them drying out. If any flowers start to appear, remove them as soon as possible to prevent them developing into seed. Ideally, you want a collection of glossy, leafy plants.

Which herbs to choose

Parsley, cilantro (coriander), and mint are fairly hardy and can survive fairly chilly conditions. Mint and lemon balm grow best by themselves because they're invasive plants and will overtake other herbs in containers.

How to dry herbs

Last year, I had an abundance of leftover herbs from my container herb garden, so I decided to dry them for storage. Not only does this provide you with a good supply of herbs over the winter, but you can also give them away as gifts. Drying works best on herbs such as bay, dill, marjoram, oregano, rosemary, and thyme that don't have a high moisture content. I start the drying process in late summer and then store my dried herbs in preserving jars.

1 Cut healthy stems from your herb plants and remove any withered or diseased leaves.

2 Wash the stems gently in cold water and pat dry with kitchen paper.

3 Remove any leaves from the bottom inch or so of the stems.

4 Bundle together about four to six stems, and tie them securely with some string or garden twine.

5 You can then dry your herbs by hanging them on a herb-drying rack if you have the space. Alternatively, place the bundle of herbs upside down in a paper bag pierced with several holes, tie the bag securely at the top with some string or garden twine, and then hang the bag in a warm, airy room.

6 Check the bag after about two weeks or so to see if your herbs are fully dried before storing them in preserving jars.

all things edible

Mint

Sweet basil

Thyme

Chive flowers

Purple sage

Moroccan mint

Purple basil

Chervil

Rosemary

I think there's nothing worse than opening the refrigerator and being greeted by a bag of limp, old salad leaves. You bought them yesterday and they failed to last the night. Also, the cost of buying bags of salad each week soon begins to add up. A much more cost-effective —and, I think, tastier—way to keep up your salad stocks is to grow your own!

SALAD CROPS

Salad crops are incredibly easy to grow on a balcony. They work well in containers with other plants because most salad varieties are shallow-rooted. They're fast-growing, so you're quick to see results, which is both rewarding and makes life easy when you want a few salad leaves for a side dish or sandwich.

Growing your salad leaves

There are also some hardy varieties available that can cope with colder temperatures, so you can even have a regular salad supply during the chilly winter months. If you're growing salads on your balcony or roof garden, you should be fairly immune to slugs and other pests that usually feast on salad leaves, unless you've inadvertently brought them up with new plants or in some potting mix.

You may want to start off your seedlings inside and then transfer them outside as they mature. When the leaves are ready to harvest, cut them off from the edge using a pair of small scissors or a knife, ensuring that you keep the actual plant undamaged. This will help to keep your lettuce growing and you'll have leaves for the entire season. These are known as cut-and-come-again salad crops.

Which varieties to choose

For a winter salad, I recommend you try mizuna, mustard leaves, and winter purslane; all three grow happily when the temperature drops. During the spring and summer, I would suggest you try romaine lettuces and looseleaf lettuces (such as 'Lollo Rosso' and 'Red Sails').

Salad Fact File

When to sow: Early spring to late summer

General care:

- Salad crops need regular watering, which should be increased in dry weather.
- Spray with diluted fertilizer if you notice any pests or diseases.

Harvesting:

- Harvest and sow little and often; usually four to five weeks after planting.
- Pick leaves around the edge of the plant to encourage new growth.

Pests and diseases:

- Downy mildew: large yellow patches appear on older leaves, and moldy areas develop on the underside of leaves; remove diseased leaves as soon as they appear.
- Grey mold: fungus turns plants a reddish-brown; often occurs during periods of high humidity; monitor closely when you water.

Scallions (spring onions) taste great in salads and work well as a garnish on lots of different dishes. These mild-tasting onions are basically young plants, which would develop into mature onions if left in the potting mix. I especially like using them in Asian soup dishes and Vietnamese summer rolls, but there are endless ways of using them in your cooking.

SCALLIONS

Scallions are easy to grow and an excellent starter plant in your new vegetable-patch container. I think they're a good choice if you are a novice and will really help boost your home-growing confidence. You can grow them successfully in containers, so they're a perfect extra on an urban balcony. Scallions don't spread out as much as some other crops and will more or less take care of themselves as they mature. You just need to check that you allow enough room between each seed when you sow.

The right growing conditions

It's a good rule of thumb when growing scallions to make sure that the potting mix is kept moist, but not soggy; you don't want to overwater the plants as this will make them rot. When you've decided to plant scallions, you might want to prepare the potting mix a few days in advance and add some solid organic fertilizer pellets to the mix. Scallions are usually ready about eight weeks after sowing. They're also hardy plants and can weather colder temperatures, making them ideal for balconies and roof gardens.

Which varieties to choose

The varieties of scallion that most people grow are 'White Lisbon' and 'White Lisbon Winter Hardy'. The latter, as its name suggests, is hardy throughout the winter. You can also buy a gorgeous variety called 'North Holland Blood Red', which has attractive, burgundy-colored bulbs.

Scallion Fact File

When to sow: Early spring to mid-summer (you'll need to sow hardy varieties such as 'White Lisbon Winter Hardy' in late summer or early fall).

General care:
- Water the plants if the weather is dry, but do not give them too much water otherwise.
- Feed occasionally with a liquid fertilizer.

Harvesting:
- Harvest from early summer to mid-fall when the bulbs are mature and the foliage turns yellow (hardy varieties can be harvested in early spring).

Pests and diseases:
- Onion fly: small flies that lay eggs on the plants; use a pesticide to deter them.
- Neck/onion white rot: different mold on onions; lift out infected plants to avoid the disease spreading.

Cook's tip
One of the reasons I like cooking with scallions is that they are much milder than normal onions, and both the green tops and the small, white bulbs are edible.

Harvesting scallions

Radishes

GROW RADISHES Radishes are an ideal crop for growing in containers. They germinate and mature quickly, making them perfect for the impatient kitchen gardener, and look and taste wonderful thinly sliced in salads. You can sow radish seeds in a container of soil-based potting mix from late winter. Once the seedlings have germinated, thin them out and use the discarded seedlings in salads. Water regularly and then harvest your radishes about five weeks after sowing. Remember, the longer you leave your radishes unharvested, the hotter they will become!

Strawberries are the urban gardener's best friend. They are easy to grow in small containers or hanging baskets, which is perfect for those with limited outdoor space. They're also simple to care for and will reward you with a repeat harvest for a few years.

STRAWBERRIES

In my opinion, supermarket strawberries are almost a different fruit to home-grown ones. Quite simply, a freshly picked strawberry is brighter, tastier, and much sweeter. They taste just like the strawberries that many of us can remember from our childhoods, when they were served with lots of sugar and cream! Your strawberry plants are great garden investments and, with a little love and care, they will provide you with fruit for a few years to come.

Growing your strawberries
With their shallow roots, strawberries grow well in small spaces, making them ideal for containers. The best way to grow most strawberries is from runners or commercially supplied plants. You can grow alpine or wild strawberries from seed, but they don't usually produce much fruit—a good tip is to put the seed in the freezer for three or four weeks before planting in early spring. This helps the seeds in the young stages of growth.

I would start off the strawberry seeds in a sunny spot indoors before putting them outside when they have three or four true leaves. Make sure that you keep the potting mix in the containers moist, but don't let it become waterlogged. It's also important to feed your strawberry plants occasionally with an organic liquid fertilizer (you could use a tomato fertilizer).

To prevent the fruit from rotting when it is in contact with the potting mix, I sometimes place a layer of straw or some slates underneath the plants. Fortunately, rotting fruit isn't such a big problem if you are growing your strawberries in smaller containers or hanging baskets.

Which varieties to choose
When growing strawberries, it's fun to experiment and try different varieties. You can also combine different types: choose from 'Elvira', which produces large fruits; alpine or wild strawberries, which have smaller berries; and 'Hapil', with large, bright red fruits.

Strawberry Fact File
When to plant: Mid-spring

General care:
• Water regularly and increase watering levels during dry spells.
• Strawberries do not require much feeding, and fertilizer should not be added after spring.

Harvesting:
• Pick any fruit as soon as it is ripe to prevent it rotting on the plant.
• Harvest in dry weather.

Pests and diseases:
• Slugs: these are attracted to the fruits; put down slug pellets or use feet on your containers.
• Birds and squirrels: these visitors enjoy eating the fruit, especially if it is in a high position; place a protective net over the plants.

GROW BLUEBERRIES This popular fruit is very much a "super food," being high in valuable antioxidants and vitamins. Plant up one blueberry plant in a large container in mid-fall. Blueberries are acid-loving plants, which means that you'll need to use an ericaceous potting mix. When planting your blueberry, add a slow-release ericaceous fertilizer to the potting mix and replenish this according to the manufacturer's instructions. Water thoroughly after planting and, if possible, use rainwater collected from a rain barrel because tap water may be too alkaline for this acid-loving plant. Water your containers regularly and harvest the berries as soon as they start ripening.

Blueberries

There's nothing worse than buying bland-tasting, watery tomatoes, which means that you have to spend a fortune on vine-ripened tomatoes to recapture the taste of the luscious fruits that you can find in the Mediterranean. Thankfully, it is both easy and rewarding to grow your own tomatoes at home.

TOMATOES

Tomato Fact File
When to sow and plant: Sow early to mid-spring; plant out in the early summer months.

General care:
● Water the roots of the plant.
● Don't overwater, as this can rot the fruit (it's better to water too little than too much).
● Water early in the day.
● Use a tomato fertilizer every couple of weeks.
● Look for fertilizer with a high phosphate and potassium content.

Harvesting:
● Pick tomatoes when brightly colored and the fruit is slightly soft to the touch, usually from mid-summer to late fall.

Pests and diseases:
● Blossom end rot: the fruit turns black; often caused by underwatering.
● Cloudy spot: prevent white or yellow patches, caused by stink bugs by using a pesticide.
● Sour rot: fruit with deep, wide cracks caused by fungus lying on the ground; make sure your plants are well supported.

Cook's tip
Try growing basil alongside your tomatoes; just add some mozzarella and you have a delicious, home-grown Caprese salad.

You can grow tomatoes in most types of container or even in growbags (there are some great surrounds made from materials such as wicker that can make them look more attractive). I would check first how large the variety you've chosen will grow before deciding on the container. Tomatoes flourish in a hot, sunny position, but don't enjoy dry conditions. Dry soil will reduce the number of fruits that are produced, but you'll have to make sure that the container has adequate drainage at the same time, otherwise the plants will rot in the soggy potting mix. As well as requiring constant watering, tomatoes also need regular feeding once the fruits have formed. Why not try some companion planting by growing marigolds, nasturtiums, or onions with the tomatoes. They all have a strong scent, which will hopefully deter fruit-eating insects?

Types of tomato
There are three main types of tomato plant, identified by the size of their fruits: cherry tomatoes; standard, or medium tomatoes; and beefsteak tomatoes. There are also variants on these such as plum tomatoes and oxheart tomatoes. Tomato plants also take different forms, including single-stemmed plants known as cordons; bush tomatoes; and trailing, or tumbling, tomatoes. Here are a few useful tips on growing the different types:

Bush tomatoes don't require much support or pinching out and will only grow to approximately 12in (30cm) in height, which means they are most suitable for large window boxes or pots. Tomato bushes tend to produce tasty plum tomatoes.

Tomato flowers

Cherry tomatoes

Vine tomatoes

Ripening tomatoes

Tumbling tomatoes will trail over the edge of a container and so are ideal for a roof garden or balcony or even a hanging basket. They often produce excellent cherry tomatoes.

Cordon tomatoes are the most popular type of tomato and are usually grown attached to a cane or string. You can also train them up a metal spiral support. You'll have to pinch out the growing tip of cordons once four trusses of fruit have appeared.

Which varieties to choose

There is a wide range of varieties to choose from. Don't feel restricted to growing salad tomatoes; you can easily expand your ingredients list and grow beefsteak tomatoes, for example. Reliable varieties include:

Cherry tomatoes: 'Gardener's Delight', 'Super Sweet 100', and 'Tumbler'
Medium tomatoes: 'Alicante', 'Moneymaker', and 'Shirley'
Beefsteak tomatoes: 'Super Marmande' and 'Supersteak'

GROW EGGPLANTS Growing other fruiting vegetables such as eggplants (aubergines) means that you can make dishes such as ratatouille with your own home-grown ingredients. It's a sensible idea to start off eggplants from seed sown in pots indoors in spring before transplanting them to a larger pot or window box filled with soil-based potting mix and moving them outside in early summer to a warm, sunny, sheltered spot. Delicious varieties include 'Baby Rosanna', 'Florida High Bush', and 'Money Maker'. Support eggplants when they get taller with some canes and string, and then pinch out the growing tips once the plants reach a heigh of 15in (38cm). Water your eggplants regularly and feed them every two weeks with a high-potash liquid feed. Harvest the eggplants from mid-summer onwards.

Eggplant & marigolds

Bell pepper

GROW BELL PEPPERS Bell peppers do not have the fiery heat of chilli peppers but still make a useful cooking ingredient. You'll need to sow your bell peppers in small pots in spring under cover, using a soil-based potting mix. Try varieties such as 'Kaibi Round' and 'Mandarin'. Peppers for outdoors will need to be hardened off in early summer before being placed outside. Make sure you keep your plants well watered and feed them with a high-potash liquid fertilizer once a week. Bell peppers may need staking with a cane and string or garden twine as they grow taller. You'll be able to harvest them from mid-spring to mid-fall.

Potato flowers

Potatoes can **easily** be grown at home in large tubs on your balcony or roof garden. **Home-grown** potatoes are much **fresher** and have a **better texture** than store-brought produce, and the **leaves** are also **bright** and **green**, providing a **lush** backdrop to other plants and crops in your urban garden.

POTATOES

Growing potatoes at home means you have a fantastic opportunity to explore and experiment with many different varieties; you can pick and choose from larger King Edward potatoes or smaller Charlotte salad potatoes, for example.

While growing potatoes at home is becoming ever more popular, remember that they do attract slugs and other garden pests, which can damage the planting (although this is not so much of a problem in elevated gardens on balconies and roofs). Similarly, weeds can interfere with the plants and stall their growth. It's possible to grow potatoes from seeds and you can even grow them from organic store-bought potatoes that have sprouted.

Do I have to "chit" my potatoes?

To get your potatoes off to a flying start, it is often recommended that you "chit" them before planting. "Chitting" simply means encouraging the seed potatoes to sprout before you plant them. This is not essential for maincrop potatoes, but it should be done if you are planning to grow first earlies (new potatoes) and salad varieties.

Each seed potato has a more rounded, blunt end (known as the rose) with a number of "eyes". You need to stand the tubers with the blunt end uppermost in a tray or an old egg box in plenty of natural light. The potatoes are ready to be planted out when the shoots are ½–1in (1.5–2.5cm) long.

Freshly harvested potatoes

"Chitting" potatoes

Healthy potato foliage

Growing your potatoes

Potatoes grow best in large containers. You can use large recycled ones such as dolly tubs, plastic tubs, or even old trash cans. I would recommend using a good potting mix and a reliable organic general-purpose fertilizer. Place your potatoes in a spot that receives plenty of sun, and water them regularly. It's important to keep the soil moist but not soggy; if it's too wet, the potatoes will rot. Often, if the moisture levels are inconsistent, you'll probably find that your potatoes will become misshapen.

You can begin to harvest your first potato crop as soon as the flowers appear on the plants. I really don't think there's anything better than reaching down, getting your hands dirty, and pulling fresh potatoes from the potting mix.

Which varieties to choose

There are lots of potato varieties to choose from. Some may be better for using in salads or for roasting or baking. Reliable varieties include:

First earlies: 'Accent', 'Red Duke of York', and 'Swift'
Second earlies: 'Charlotte', 'Estima', and 'Kestrel'
Maincrop potatoes: 'Desirée', 'King Edward', and 'Picasso'.

Potato Fact File

When to plant: Mid- to late spring

General care:

● Potatoes need to be watered well.
● After blossoms appear on the plant, it's best to increase the water supply.
● Feed potatoes two weeks after planting with a fertilizer high in potassium and phosphate.

Harvesting:

● Harvest earlies when the potato plant is flowering (usually around mid-summer for first earlies, and late summer for second earlies) and maincrops 15 days after the plants have finished flowering.

Pests and diseases:

● Potato blight: dark blotches on the leaves; best to remove all foliage.
● Common scab: patches of corky-looking tissue on plants; these plants are thirsty, so keep up your watering regime.

GROW CARROTS Although carrots are best grown in the open ground, you can try growing short-rooted types such as 'Mignon' and 'Parmex' in containers in your sky-high kitchen garden. Use a soil-based potting mix (with some added general-purpose fertilizer and horticultural grit because carrots prefer a light, sandy soil) and sow the seed thinly from mid-spring. If you are using a large container, why not sow the seed in rows, 6in (15cm) apart, as you would in a vegetable patch? Thin the seedlings when they are large enough to handle, leaving about 3in (8cm) between each one. Harvest your carrots about eight weeks later. Watch out for carrot root fly, which is attracted by the scent of the foliage and lays its eggs on the plant in late spring and can badly damage your crop. The carrot root can also split if watering is irregular, so keep up a consistent watering routine.

Harvesting carrots

ZUCCHINI

Zucchini (courgettes) are a great way to fill your containers because they grow and spread rapidly. They have large, **bright** flowers and big leaves that provide a great **background** for displaying the other plants in your small urban space to great **advantage**.

If you are a novice gardener, zucchini are a great vegetable to grow and you'll probably find that they will also prove one of the most productive in your urban garden. I should point out that they can grow quite large (which may be something to bear in mind if you only have a small balcony), but there are some great varieties to choose from that are perfect for containers if you start them off from seed.

Growing your zucchini

Like most vegetables, zucchini enjoy a sunny, sheltered spot away from the wind. They're not fond of chilly temperatures, so avoid planting them toward the end of winter when there is still a risk of frost. You could always start your zucchini seedlings indoors in smaller pots and, once the plants have matured and it's slightly warmer outside, you can transfer them to an outdoor container.

It's important to use a free-draining potting mix because you will need to water your zucchini regularly. When the flowers start appearing and the fruits start to swell, it's crucial to keep watering the plants. This will probably happen when the weather is warmer and the plants are thirsty. Also watch out for slugs! They really love zucchini, so I would suggest using either copper feet on your containers, or copper rings around the base. Another trick is to use crushed eggshells, although I have not had such great results with this method. Harvest the zucchini as soon as they reach a usable size (normally between 4–6in/10–15cm).

Which varieties to choose

You can grow yellow as well as green zucchini. Green varieties include 'All Green Bush', 'Nero Milan', and 'Patio Star'. Reliable yellow varieties include 'Buckingham' and 'Jemma F1'.

COOKING WITH FLOWERS Zucchini were one of the first vegetables I grew because I was particularly interested in getting hold of some of the flowers to cook with. Personally, I think that the flowers are the best part of the plant because they are a great delicacy (which you cannot buy readily) and fantastic for a dinner-party appetizer to wow your friends.

Zucchini Fact File

When to sow and plant: Sow late sprint to early summer; plant out in the early summer.

General care:

• Plenty of water is essential, especially when the plant is flowering. Apply liquid feed regularly.

Harvesting:

• Harvest the fruit three times a week at the height of the growing season.
• Some varieties are ready after eight weeks.
• Cut the stems attaching the fruit to the plant rather than breaking them off.

Pests and diseases:

• Slugs: use feet on containers to prevent slugs gaining access to the pots or sprinkle salt or crushed eggshells around the plants.
• Cucumber mosaic: spread by insects and eventually turns the leaves yellow; best to dig up rotted plants to prevent the infection spreading.

CHAPTER 5

ENJOYING YOUR BALCONY

So, you have your outdoor planting mastered and put in
all the ground work. Now, it's time to sit back and
enjoy! Let's turn our thoughts to giving your garden
an inviting ambience by adding those all-important
decorative touches to turn your urban space into the
ultimate balcony garden. From summer barbecues to
tables and chairs for nocturnal dining, adding those
finishing flourishes will make even the smallest of
spaces work for you.

Balconies and roof gardens located in urban areas can seem rather dull and gray because they are frequently surrounded by concrete walls and have uninspiring inner city views. Once you have selected and planted your containers, you can then use a range of different accessories, from tables and chairs to hammocks and recliners to help soften your balcony or roof-garden space and give it a unified look.

FURNISHINGS

WHAT TO USE

Astroturf

Bistro-style tables and chairs

Deckchairs

Hammocks

Paint effects

Relaxing recliners

Selection of cushions and throws

Vintage and recycled containers

There are plenty of interesting ways in which to adorn your balcony or roof garden, from selecting distinctive furniture to adding a few decorative accessories. There are a few points to bear in mind to ensure that your outdoor furniture retains its look and remains durable. For example, be sure to pick out pieces that won't fade or crack in the sun and will also be sturdy enough to withstand the blustery conditions that inevitably come with an elevated space.

Decorative effects

Vintage pieces such as birdhouses, glass lanterns, interesting jars, and small bottles all work well and will give your balcony garden a unique look. I provide more advice in chapter 3, on planting up unusual and recycled containers. Other effective ideas include converting the balcony or roof terrace into an elevated green space by using Astroturf to cover up ugly-looking concrete floors (see pages 46–47). Another decorative option is to paint the walls in a different color. Simply consider the atmosphere or look you are hoping to create and select the paint color accordingly. For example, if you wish to create a Mediterranean vibe, why not paint a wall in a rich terracotta and coordinate it with your pots? There are plenty of creative options to choose from to give your balcony or roof garden a personal signature.

How to look after outdoor furniture

● Invest in a lightweight, waterproof cover to protect your balcony furniture in cold weather.

● Fasten down furniture or bring it inside during windy spells if your balcony or roof garden is on a high level.

● Wipe down metal outdoor furniture regularly with a damp cloth and check for signs of rust. Any rusty areas need to be sanded down and repainted.

● Preserve wooden furniture by revarnishing it annually and check for wood rot.

Seating and accessories

One of the easiest ways to make your balcony more comfortable is to add a few chairs and cushions. Choose cushions that reflect some of the colors you've used in your containers and planting. You can either alternate the shades or blend in the hues. Try different fabrics and textures. If the balcony is small, matching the cushions to ones used indoors will help to create a small outdoor room.

A **wonderful** benefit of having your own balcony or roof garden is being able to use it for entertaining and hosting **parties** outside. City apartments can be rather small, so it's great to be able to use the outside space for social occasions. In the summer months, you can keep a **barbecue** outside for long, lazy **afternoon** and in the fall, you can watch **fireworks** light up the night sky from the comfort of your own elevated space.

PREPARING FOR PARTIES

WHAT TO USE

Barbecue

Bunting

Cushions and tablecloths

Decorative features (large candles and lanterns)

Fairy lights

Glass jars filled with pretty flowers

Ice-box for drinks

Seed-packet gifts

Vintage cups and saucers

There will be times when you simply wish to entertain a few friends at home on your balcony or roof terrace. However, on occasions, you may be having a barbecue or throwing an evening party and really want to make an impression. Paying a little extra attention to the lighting, accessories and finishing touches will make all the difference.

Barbecues and afternoon teas

A barbecue in the summer need not be restricted to gardens. Simply look out for a small barbecue that is not too cumbersome (you can now buy some great little barbecues that fold up flat). Check the manufacturer's safety recommendations first and make sure you place the barbecue in a suitable spot. During the afternoon, pick some edible ingredients from your window boxes and containers that you can barbecue or use in salads. For an outside afternoon tea party with a vintage look, some bunting makes a wonderful addition to the balcony. There are plenty of different colors, prints, and patterns to choose from that will set off your flowers and plants. Use cake-stands as table centerpieces and pick mismatching vintage cups and saucers; miniature cupcakes look pretty placed on antique wire-stands. Finally, I would choose pretty cushion covers and tablecloths to finish the vintage look, perhaps coordinating them with the bunting. Another choice for table decorations is to pick some cuttings from your containers and place them in glass jars.

MAKING GUESTS FEEL WELCOME A few tea-lights and a freshly prepared meal will do much to create a memorable evening and really make your guests feel special. If you are throwing an evening party, then why not pick ingredients that you have grown yourself to use when making delicious cocktails? If you want to prepare in advance, then you can freeze edible cuttings such as mint and then use them later in your party food and drink.

Evening parties

For an evening party, it's important to think about the lighting. Decorating your space with fairy lights will create a magical look for summer parties. Think about where to hang the lights (they shouldn't get in the way of your guests), as well as which areas of the balcony need to be lit. Colorful paper lanterns also look fantastic for birthday parties. They're very pretty and look charming fluttering in the wind; you can even weave flowers through the lanterns.

A great finishing touch for your balcony garden is lighting, especially for entertaining or enjoying your balcony in the evening. Lighting creates an enchanting night-time garden. What could be more magical than sitting outside after dusk and gazing out over the city rooftops? Good lighting will do much to set the mood and create a soothing ambience.

LIGHTING

There are plenty of lighting options to choose from, so consider whether you'll be using your balcony as an extension of your apartment or as a separate outside space? A lighting challenge that often faces the balcony gardener is the lack of outdoor power sockets. You can either trail an extension lead through a window or use environmentally friendly solar-powered lamps. Nowadays, there are plenty of well-designed solar lamps to choose from. I use a few in different areas to draw the attention and light different plantings. When placing the solar lamps, play around with different heights and arrangements. For instance, you might group a few lights around one plant and then scatter a few through other plants. Instead of solar lights, you can also use renewable batteries in other lighting devices that work outside.

An important factor to consider is the proximity of your neighbors. Soft lighting is always the best choice for this reason or you could even invest in outdoor floor-track lighting. If your balcony is covered by a roof, why not choose a lantern as a dramatic centerpiece to hang over your table and chairs? Small, solar-powered LED lights or fairy lights also look very pretty hanging over railings and threaded through trees.

For entertaining, I think there's nothing prettier than candles and small lanterns. You can also theme your lighting; a Moroccan dinner, for instance, could be lit with metal lattice Moroccan lanterns. If you're by water, wicker ball string lights give a nautical feel.

HANGING VOTIVE CANDLES

These votive candles are very simple to make. It may take you a few attempts to get them right (it certainly did in my case), but please persevere because they are definitely worth the effort.

1 Cut a 16–20in (40–50cm) length of wire, depending on whether you want to hang your glass jar from a long or short loop. Then, create a small loop in the wire, about a third of the way along. Wrap the wire tightly around the rim of the jar, making sure that the two ends of the wire cross over opposite the loop.

2 Secure the wire in position by twisting the wire ends over each other, thus creating a hook. Cut off one length of the wire, leaving just enough wire to pull over to the other side in order to make a handle. Push the end of the wire through the hook.

3 Finally, use your fingers or cutting pliers to bend the wire to secure it in place. Cut off any excess wire. You can then place a tea-light in the jar to illuminate your balcony or roof garden with a subtle light.

WHAT YOU NEED

Preserving jar or any small glass jar

Silver or copper pliable wire

Pair of cutting pliers

Tea-light

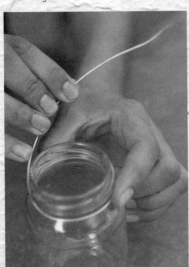
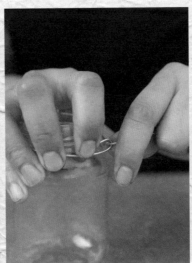
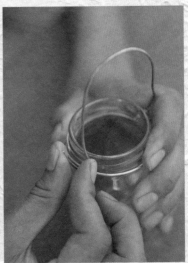

Gardeners can create simple, **inexpensive** and **creative** gifts that can be used either as **party** favors or **gifts** that you can take with you when visiting a friend's house. It's a **lovely** way for others to remember an **enjoyable** visit to your balcony garden and to grow a little **keepsake** of their own when they get home.

GROWING FOR GIFTS

WHAT TO USE

Brown paper for wrapping and packaging

Colorful ribbons

Name labels and string

Raffia in different colors

Seed packets (of both ornamental and edible plants)

Selection of home-grown produce (such as runner beans or chilli peppers)

Small cardboard presentation boxes

Small plants for planting (such as baby ferns, ivy, and conifers)

Storage jars for planting up

Terracotta pots

Tissue paper

A great way to share a part of your balcony garden is to give plants, cuttings, and edible produce as gifts. There are lots of different and imaginative ways to present handmade gifts and you can also personalize them for your friends by writing or printing labels with the recipient's name.

Giving edible gifts

If you grow edible produce on your balcony or roof garden, why not package it imaginatively to create a unique gift for guests? You can wrap runner beans, for example, in some brown paper and then tie this into a bundle with brightly colored raffia. Alternatively, you could match the dramatic color of a red chilli pepper wrapped in brown paper to a name label for your guest. Use personalized name labels with messages for your friends or use the label to tell your friend where the produce comes from. If you're planning to entertain on your balcony, what could be better than giving your guests a bespoke party favor like this and sharing the delights of your garden?

Other gift ideas for friends and guests

● Plants ivies or spring bulbs in cardboard letter boxes. If you are presenting a few plants in a collection of boxes, then why not choose letters that spell out the names of your guests?

● Give vintage or prettily decorated seed packets containing ornamental or edible plant seed for your guests to grow at home. Tie the packets with matching ribbons.

● Small plants such as succulents grown in a little potting mix in an old jam jar. These can look beautiful kept on the desk in a home office and will remind your guests of a memorable evening.

Wrapped runner beans

Gifts in glass jars

Planted letter boxes

Pretty seed packet presents

TERRACOTTA TERRARIUMS

It's easy to create your own small terrariums as gifts. They are inexpensive to put together using recycled materials and make lovely presents. These cuttings are simply planted in pots under handmade terrariums.

WHAT YOU NEED

Small terracotta pots

Small plastic bottles

Cutting potting mix

Selection of cuttings (such as pelargoniums)

Hormone rooting powder

Natural raffia or baker's string

Labels and craft pegs

1 Find some old plastic bottles to make your homemade terrariums. You need to make sure they are clear and watertight so that they will provide a removable and secure cover. Plastic bottles like these are simple to use and will give your plants great protection. Cut off the bottom of each plastic bottle and remove the caps. Fill each small terracotta pot with some potting mix suitable for growing cuttings, and use a stick or dibber to insert a hole in the mix.

2 Take your cuttings from the parent plant (see page 24). Although many plants root quickly without any help, it's worthwhile using some hormone rooting powder to make sure that they do. The cuttings can then be taken as close as a week before your social event. Make sure you select a strong, healthy plant to take a cutting from. It has to have enough stems to ensure that taking a few cuttings will not kill the parent plant. Dip the end of your cutting into the rooting powder and then lower it gently into the hole in the potting mix. Firm in carefully with your fingertips before watering in.

3 Position the plastic-bottle terrarium over the cutting and push down very gently so that the bottle is anchored in the potting mix.

ADDING FINISHING TOUCHES If you are giving the terrarium as a gift, why not decorate it in some way? I suggest you tie raffia or string around the top of the bottle in a color that suits your friend's style or the color of the plant. You can then clip a message or name label to the plastic bottle using a tiny craft peg.

A wonderful way to **celebrate** the start of spring and the end of the coldest months of the year is by planting a fresh new window box and using **bright spring** colors. This spring window box would make a lovely **seasonal gift** and you can, of course, also **decorate** the display to give it an Easter theme.

SPRING WINDOW BOX

For this window box, I chose some cat grass with a few planted "egglings" sitting on top. Cat grass has vivid green leaves that are perfect for spring, but you can also use wheat grass. Start off the plants in small clay pots in a sunny spot indoors and water them every other day. Add Epsom salts to the water about once a week to stimulate growth. Once the cat grass is established, trim the leaves regularly.

Eggshells make great mini-containers to start off seedlings. To prepare your eggshell, knock off the top, remove the contents, and wash well. Fill with damp potting mix. Make a dent in the center and sprinkle in a few seeds. Cover with mix and moisten with a few water drops, ensuring the water is all absorbed before adding more.

Tying with raffia as a gift

YOU WILL NEED

Metal slatted
window box

Moss for lining

Potting mix (plus a
seed potting mix for
the "egglings")

Cat (or wheat) grass

Selection of seeds

Duck eggs

OTHER SPRING PLANTING IDEAS Plan ahead and plant
bulbs in the fall for a spring display. Tulips, daffodils,
and hyacinths are all lovely spring flowers that are easy
to care for. Why not mix the bulbs with some green grasses;
shades of yellow, blue, and purple look great planted
against this bright green backdrop. When planting bulbs,
try to keep the box inside for a while, and water regularly
before moving it outdoors as the weather gets warmer.

Flowering and **blossoming** window boxes aren't simply for the summer. There are numerous plants and **flowers** to choose from that will grow well during the **cooler months** of the year. A fall window box is a great way to continue your summer gardening **hobby,** as the soil is still fairly warm and moist and makes a great base for **new planting.**

CONTAINERS FOR FALL

WHAT TO PLANT

Annuals (such as petunia and verbena)

Capsicums

Heather plants

Hebes

Herbs (such as sage, parsley, and thyme)

Ivy

Moss (as a finish)

Ornamental cabbages

Pumpkins

Silver *Calocephalus*

A fall window box is a wonderful way to ensure you have a celebration of seasonal color on your balcony as the summer fades away. However, it's important to know in advance what plants will survive and thrive during the fall and winter. Your summer plants may have run their course or you can replant and feed them in order to coax them into lasting into the fall. You may, however, have to protect more delicate plants during the colder months. I would recommend that you leave your fall planting until after the summer conditions have passed and there have been a few ground frosts.

The rich and vibrant colors of the fall look great planted in rustic wicker window boxes, wooden crates, and old drawers. You'll find that pumpkins, ornamental cabages, and certain capsicums will all grow well in containers and can also be planted up in time for Halloween parties. There are also plenty of annuals to choose from for your fall planting: petunias will perform well until the first frosts, and the colors range from whites and yellows to reds and purples. Verbenas grow equally well in window boxes and are hardy during the fall. Ivy is a popular foliage plant for containers and available in a selections of colors, ranging from dark green to silver, while herbs such as thyme, parsley, and sage are recommended if you are looking for hardy plants.

16

OTHER FALL PLANTING IDEAS Fall is also a great time to feature shrubs and bulbs. Consider shrubs such as hebe and *Euonymus europaeus* 'Red Cascade', which has fiery red leaves and berries in the fall. Also try heathers: the flowers never fully open and will not die until pollinated, so they can last for months. Fall bulbs include crocus with clusters of lilac flowers.

Hebe & ornamental cabbages
planted in an old drawer

These festive displays will add a real touch of glamor and Christmas cheer to your garden or home. This wonderful window-box display creates a winter wonderland by day and a warming view by night when illuminated with candles. And what better way to greet your guest than with this stylish edible Christmas wreath adorning your front door?

CHRISTMAS DECORATIONS

WHAT TO USE

For the window box

Chamaecyparis
and heathers

Slate chippings

Fake snow, garland,
pine cones, and baubles

For the table display

Holly, ivy, and
pine cones

Tea-light lanterns

A fabulous way to decorate your balcony or home is to make this evocative Christmas window box. Using three dwarf *Chamaecyparis* gives the effect of a festive woodland forest and creates an idyllic winter scene. The box can be elegantly presented as part of a table display outdoors or used as an indoor decoration. I collected together pine cones and lots of little vintage glass baubles, and also scattered fake snow to give a glistening effect. A red garland creates a shocking impact juxtaposed with the surrounding moody browns and greens. For a night-time display, use an array of tea-ight lanterns to cast a warm glow that sparkles on the snow.

Why not make this a project for children by adding Christmas toys such as reindeers, Santa Claus, elves, and also sacks of presents; it will make a great alternative to the traditional Nativity scene.

MAKE A CHRISTMAS WREATH You can use a florist's wreath with floral foam to make an elegant Christmas decoration. I chose four herbs so that I could divide the circle into quarters. Use woody-stemmed herbs such as sage, thyme, lavender, and rosemary as their sturdiness makes them easier to push into the foam. Soak the foam first before inserting the stalks. Hang the wreath securely on your front door.

Christmas herb wreath

JOURNAL

Spring

Summer

Fall

Winter

PLANT LIST

Delphiniums and roses

Balloon flower (*Platycodon*)
Basil (*Ocimum basilicum*)
Basil mint (*Mentha x piperita citrata* 'Basil')
Bell pepper (*Capsicum annuum* Grossum Group)
Black bamboo (*Phyllostachys nigra*)
Blackcurrant sage (*Salvia microphylla* var. *microphyla*)
Blueberry (*Vaccinium corybosum*)
Borage (*Borago officinalis*)
Box (*Buxus sempervirens*)
Bronze fennel (*Foeniculum vulgare* 'Purpureum')
Bush basil (*Ocimum minimum*)
Butterfly bush (*Buddleja davidii*)
Cabbage (*Brassica oleracea* Capitata Group)
Carrot (*Daucus carota*)
Cat grass (*Avena sativa*)
Catmint (*Nepeta*)
Chamomile (*Matricaria recutita*)
Chervil (*Anthriscus cerefolium*)
Chilli pepper (*Capsicum annuum* Longum Group)
Chives (*Allium schoenoprasum*)
Cilantro/coriander (*Coriandrum sativum*)
Climbing hydrangea (*Hydrangea petiolaris*)
Coneflower (*Echinacea*)

Cornflower (*Centaurea cyanus*)
Curly-leaved parsley (*Petroselinum crispum*)
Daffodil (*Narcissus*)
Dill (*Anethum graveolens*)
Dogwood (*Cornus*)
Eggplant/aubergine (*Solanum melongena*)
English lavender (*Lavandula angustifolia*)
English mace (*Achillea ageratum*)
Fennel (*Foeniculum vulgare*)
Flat-leaved parsley (*Petroselinum crispum neapolitanum*)
Foxglove (*Digitalis*)
French lavender (*Lavandula stoechas*)
Garlic (*Allium sativum*)
Garlic chives (*Allium tuberosum*)
Ginger (*Zingiber officinale*)
Globe artichoke (*Cynara cardunculus* Scolymus Group)
Golden bamboo (*Phyllostachys aurea*)
Golden marjoram (*Origanum vulgare* 'Aureum')
Hambury root parsley (*Petroselinum crispum* Radicosum Group)
Hare's tail (*Lagurus ovatus*)
Heath or ling (*Erica*)

Sempervivums

French lavender

Heather (*Calluna vulgaris*)
Holly (*Ilex*)
Holy basil (*Ocimum tenuifolium*)
Hyacinth (*Hyacinthus*)
Ivy (*Hedera*)
Jasmine (*Jasminum*)
Kaffir lime (*Citrus hystrix*)
Kumquat (*Citrus japonica*)
Laurel (*Laurus nobilis*)
Lemon balm (*Melissa officinalis*)
Lemon grass (*Cymbopogon citratus*)
Lemon thyme (*Thymus citriodorus*)
Lettuce (*Latuca sativa*)
Lilac (*Syringa*)
Lily (*Lilium*)
Lupin (*Lupinus*)
Marigold (*Tagetes*)
Mind-your-own-business (*Soleirolia soleirolii*)
Mint (*Mentha*)
Mizuna (*Brassica rapa* var. *japonica*)
Moroccan mint (*Mentha spicata* 'Moroccan')
Mustard leaves (*Brassica juncea*)
Orange-scented thyme (*Thymus fragrantissimus*)
Oregano (*Origanum vulgare*)
Ornamental cabbage (*Brassica oleracea*)
Pale galingale (*Cyperus eragrostis*)
Passionflower (*Passiflora*)
Peppermint (*Mentha* x *piperita*)
Potato (*Solanum tuberosum*)

Primrose (*Primula vulgaris*)
Pumpkin (*Cucurbita maxima*)
Purple smoke bush (*Cotinus coggygria* 'Royal Purple')
Radish (*Raphanus sativus*)
Red fountain grass (*Pennisetum setaceum* 'Rubrum')
Red-stemmed apple mint (*Mentha* x *gracilis* 'Madalene Hill')
Rose (*Rosa*)
Rosemary (*Rosmarinus officinalis*)
Runner beans (*Phaseolus coccineus*)
Sage (*Salvia officinalis*)
Scabious (*Scabiosa*)
Scallion/spring onion (*Allium cepa*)
Scirpus cernuus
Sea holly (*Eryngium maritima*)
Shallot (*Allium cepa* var. *aggregatum*)
Snapdragon (*Antirrhinum*)
Snowberry (*Vaccinium*)
Sorrel (*Rumex acetosa*)
Squirrel tail grass (*Hordeum jubatum*)
Star anise (*Illicium verum*)
Strawberry (*Fragaria* x *ananassa*)
Summer savory (*Satureja hortensis*)
Sunflower (*Helianthus annuus*)
Sweet bay (*Laurus nobilis*)
Sweet bell pepper (*Capsicum* species)
Sweet marjoram (*Origanum majorana*)
Sweet pea (*Lathyrus odoratus*)
Tarragon (*Artemisia dracunculus*)
Tea plant (*Camellia sinensis*)
Thyme (*Thymus vulgaris*)
Tomato (*Lycopersicon esculentum*)
Tulip (*Tulipa*)
Violet (*Viola odorata*)
Water hyacinth (*Eicchornia crassipes*)
Water lettuce (*Pistia stratioides*)
Waterlily (*Nymphaea*)
Wild arugula/rocket (*Diplotaxis tenuifolia*)
Winter purslane (*Claytonia perfoliata*)
Winter savory (*Satureja montana*)
Zucchini/courgette (*Cucurbita pepo*)

GLOSSARY

Alkaline This is soil that has a pH level of more than 7; sometimes referred to as "sweet soil" by gardeners and farmers.

Alpine Plants that have adapted to growing in mountainous and rocky conditions.

Annual A plant that completes its lifecycle in one season.

Bedding plants These are often annuals and are suitable for growing in containers. They tend to be quick-growing and have colorful flowers.

Biennial A plant that completes its lifecycle in two seasons.

Bolt Cold-season annual plants that go to flower and seed when exposed to warm temperatures.

Bulb Plants that have underground, fleshy storage structures.

Bush A small shrub with no main stems.

Climbers Vine-like or rambling plants that will grow or creep on or over structures such as trellis.

Cloche A transparent cover used to protect plants, often in cold-weather conditions.

Coir Made from coconut husks, coir is an environmental replacement for peat moss, potting mix, and other mulches.

Creepers Plants that make long shoots and grow along the ground such as creeping fig or ivy.

Cut back Trimming a plant to encourage new growth.

Cutting A piece of a plant (whether a leaf, stem, root, or bud) that is cut from the parent plant to form a new plant.

Dead-heading The removal of faded flowers that have already bloomed; dead-heading promotes continued blooming.

Drainage Describes how water moves through the soil; all soils need good drainage to avoid plant rot.

Drill A shallow hole into which seed is sown.

Evergreen Refers to plants that keep their leaves all year round; occasionally leaves may die and fall.

Fertilizer The use of organic or inorganic plant foods, which may be in granule or liquid form, to improve the quality of soil for plant growth.

Frost The condensation and freezing of moisture in the air. Tender plants are at risk from frost and the accompanying cold temperatures.

Frost hardy Plants (usually evergreens) that are able to survive cold winter frosts without damage to their leaves.

Fungicide A chemical used to protect against, restrict, or kill plant diseases caused by fungi.

Germinate The beginnings of growth in seeds.

Hardy annual An annual plant that can withstand freezing temperatures.

Houseplants Plants that are grown and raised indoors in containers.

Insecticide A synthetic or organic chemical used to kill or repel insects.

Invasive Plants that spread quickly and crowd out other plants.

Organic Fertilizers and chemicals that have been derived from a source that is or has been alive.

Peat Remains of dead bog plants or moss that are rich in nutrients and retain water well.

Peat moss The remains of different mosses; can be used as a water-retentive addition to soil, but can alter the soil's acidity.

Perennial A plant that lives for more than one season; often more than three years under normal conditions.

Perlite Volcanic rock granules that are mixed with potting soil to improve drainage and promote moisture retention.

Pesticide A substance used to control or kill pests such as insects and also weeds.

Pollination The transfer of pollen from the anther to the stigma; this results in the formation of the seed.

Potting mix Pre-packaged soil mixture that often contains sand, garden compost, and peat moss.

Pruning The process of cutting off leaves or branches to remove dead, damaged, or diseased foliage or branches.

Rootball The network of roots (including the soil) attached to a plant.

Root hormone A chemical in powder or liquid form, which is often used to encourage seedlings to take root.

Rust A reddish-brown discoloration on plants.

Seedling A young plant in the early stages of growing from seed.

Shrub A woody plant with a framework of branches and little or no central stem.

Sowing The scattering and planting of seeds.

Species A group of similar but individual plants that are bred together and have the same distinctive features.

Succulents Plants with leaves and/or stems that are thick, fleshy, and very watery. They often have waxy outer layers, allowing the plants to retain moisture well.

Sun-shade plants These are plants that grow best in a shaded area away from the sun.

Topiary The art of clipping and training woody plants such as box to form different shapes and patterns.

Trailing plants Those that grow long stems along the ground and often root as they go. Strawberries are a good example.

Variegated leaves These are leaves that are marked or mottled with different colors.

Water garden A man-made pool formed to grow and house aquatic plants.

Wildlife plants Herbaceous plants that grow and reproduce without help or cultivation from man.

SUPPLIERS

United Kingdom

Anthropologie
00800 00268476
www.anthropologie.co.uk
*Bird trinket boxes, terracotta
colored lanterns*

Baileys
01989 561931
www. baileyshomeandgarden.com
*Outdoor accessories,
vintage tools*

The Balcony Gardener
020 74315553
www.thebalconygardener.com
*One-stop shop for your small
garden needs, containers, furniture,
tools, outdoor accessories, seeds,
kids' gardening*

Broste
(+45) 363 90300
www.brostecph.com
*Baskets, glassware, accessories,
planters*

Graham & Green
01225 418 200
www.grahamandgreen.co.uk
*Mexican chairs, parasols, bamboo
floor lanterns*

Green Tulip
01380 820 008
www.greentulip.co.uk
Bright bamboo bowls

IKEA
(see website for outlet telephone
numbers)
www.ikea.com
*Accessories, terracotta pots,
glassware*

Jennifer Newman
0203 621 5208
www.jennifernewman.com
Metal powder-coated furniture

Le Petit Jardin
01892 541152
www.le-petit-jardin.com
Colorful metal outdoor furniture

The Linen Works
020 3744 1020
www.thelinenworks.com
*Linen tablecloths, napkins, clay-
colored tableware*

Lulu & Nat
07527 812260
www.luluandnat.com
Block-printed textiles

Rastall & Daughters
01529 400545
www.rastallanddaughters.com
Christmas decorations, garlands

Pale and Interesting
01797 344077
www.paleandinteresting.com
Accessories, vintage furniture

Pedlars
01244 784 187
www.pedlars.co.uk
*Outdoor accessories, melamine
plates, glassware*

Tinsmiths
01531 632083
www.shop.tinsmiths.co.uk
*Outdoor clocks, cushions,
accessories*

Re
01434 634567
www.re-foundobjects.com
*Cushions, glassware, hand-painted
cans, accessories*

Rockett St George
01444 253391
www.rockettstgeorge.co.uk
*White candelabra, fairy lights,
decorative accessories*

Sarah Raven
0345 092 0283
www.sarahraven.com
*Glass teapot, garden tools, colored
raffia*

Six Inch
(+32) 3 609 57 02
www.sixinch.be
Yellow Louis-style outdoor chair

Susan Bradley
07905 484542
www.susanbradley.co.uk
Metal outdoor damask wallpaper

United States and Canada

Anthropologie (across USA)
(800) 309-2500
www.anthropologie.com
Ornate garden accessories and homeware

Ben Wolff, Connecticut
(860)-480-7765
www.benwolffpottery.com
Traditional and modern pottery

Flora Grubb, San Francisco
(415) 626-7256
www.floragrubb.com
Planted containers, sky planters, wall ornaments

Grdn, Brooklyn, New York
(718) 797-3628
www.grdnbklyn.com
A complete shop for the urban gardener

Jayson, Chicago
(800) 472-1885
www.jaysonhome.com
Reclaimed pots and planters, plants, container planting

Potted, Los Angeles
(323) 665-3801
www.pottedstore.com
Bright furniture, water gardens, garden decorations

Pottery Barn (across USA)
(888) 779-5176
www.potterybarn.com
Outdoor lighting, garden furniture, outdoor tableware

Pure Modern (online)
(800) 563-0593
www.puremodern.com
Outdoor, contemporary lighting

Rolling Greens, Culver City and Los Angeles
(310) 559-8656
www.rollinggreensnursery.com
Plants, containers, vintage furniture, bird feeders

Terrain at Styers, Pennsylvania
(877) 583-7724
www.shopterrain.com
Outdoor furniture, planters, plants, accessories

West Elm (across USA)
(888) 922-4119
www.westelm.com
Outdoor furniture, garden cushions, umbrella

INDEX

ACKNOWLEDGMENTS

So where do I begin? First and foremost, thank you to the wonderful team at Cico Books, especially to Cindy Richards for giving me this amazing opportunity. Sally Powell, Dawn Bates, Caroline West, and Ashley Western for their commitment and enthusiasm, and who helped make this, my first book, something I am hugely proud of.

A heart-felt thank you to Keiko Oikawa and Amanda D'Arcy for their beautiful photography, and Marisa Daly for all your hard work and gorgeous styling.

To my amazing family, words do not do justice to the incredible support they have given me throughout and always. My wonderful Mother and Father who helped facilitate all of my dreams with their endless love and kindness—not to mention the loan of their much-loved garden and putting up with all the disruption. Nicholas for being a fabulous Brother, a big thank you for your lifting and removal skills. My wonderful, ingenious Grandfather who is also my Chief Fixer and DIY assistant! And last but not least my Uncle, Michael Homer.

To the amazing TBG team Madeline Carrick and Patricia Gill for their tireless work, I could not have done it without you and I promise we will have our celebration dinner soon...

And finally, thank you to all of my brilliant friends, but especially to Sharonne, Elin, Venetia, and Abigail for all of their help, love, and support.